CRIES
OF A
MOTHER

BRENDA CAMPBELL

WORKBOOK PRESS LLC
187 E Warm Springs Rd,
Suite B285, Las Vegas, NV 89119, USA

Website: https://workbookpress.com/
Hotline: 1-888-818-4856
Email: admin@workbookpress.com

Ordering Information:
Quantity sales. Special discounts are available on quantity purchases by corporations, associations, and others. For details, contact the publisher at the address above.

Library of Congress Control Number:
ISBN-13:   978-1-957618-50-0 (Paperback Version)
                    978-1-957618-51-7 (Digital Version)

REV. DATE: 02/02/2022

A MOTHER'S CRIES

BY: BRENDA CAMPBELL

CHAPTER 1

MY DAUGHTER'S INTRODUCTION

I have lost two children's while walking through the valley of death. I looked at their death in different angles. As I sit high on this mountain top, I decided to psychologically explain my daughter's death. I'm sure you have heard every mother who has lost a child explains how unbearable and very excruciating the pain is. well, it's true I have some medicine for you to take if you are in the state of mind. Let's just start off with one capsule of Matthew 24:13 but he that shall endure unto the end, the same shall be saved. I hope that makes you feel better. Let's keep it a moving. We can't sit on this mountain together. We have to pass one valley; we now have one more so we can get to the other side. Let's walk and talk. My daughter was born April 19 1987. My daughter was a blessing to me despite the despite the fact that I was only fifteen years old. I named her Lafreshia Lanet Green.

She was so perfect and she was worth the nine months of uncertainty, and embarrassment her dad put me through I accepted the fact that I was going to raised her as a single mother. I accepted the fact that I let my daughter down by not having a real family and a broken one, I never knew things were going to be hard but I never imagined just eight months later rushing my daughter into the emergency room with fever so high. The story a mother's cries.

The day of April 19,1987 life was so precious thee almighty high had sent me a gift from heaven he sent me an angle from above that life came un expected to me Lafreshia weighted six pounds and eight oz. she was eight months old to anybody she was an ordinary baby she

1

was happy and very playful active what you can see is that she battled with a condition known as hydrocephalus everyday to explain what I'm talking about hydrocephalus is a condition in which the ventricles in the brain cannot property drain cerebrospinal fluids from the head the results are swelling of the ventricles which in the turn places pressures on the brain some of the effects in resulting in my daughter Lafreshia condition included headache nausea vomiting sleepiness and imitability her brain is stress is a direct result of my daughter Lafreshia problem with me as a mother being so young giving birth she was born on time it turned out to be a blessing unearned and unbeknown to the doctors my daughter Lafreshia suffered from the bleeding in the brain which resulted indirect consequences as it turned out this bleeding was a primary factor in my daughter Lafreshia hydrocephalus. Meaning there are water on the brain of Lafreshia and she spent months and days in the hospital my daughter had her first surgery and a week later went back in for second surgery for a shunt permanent to be placed in her head for the rest of her life.

The shunt was placed in her head the neurosurgeons that would allow her ventricles to be open unfortunately her ventricles never open so a permanent shunt had to be inserted between my daughter skull and her skin after that she would have recover and that would take a long time because she was only eight months. So that would be a journey for her it was so sadden to me, all I could do is cry because it was nothing that I could to take the pain from my daughter so hard.

Now all I could think about is her condition and her health as a mother I never thought with a blink of an eye my daughter would take a turned for the worse I just could not believe it. I just could not image and believe the horrible experience that had burned my memory and scared me this day was the worst day in my life for me thing This story changed my life forever in early January 1987 it all started a night I would never ever forget barely making to the hospital. I welcome my daughter Lafreshia Lanet green at 8:30 am on Easter day leading up to that day.

I was so anxious to meet my healthy daughter she was so precious she came so fast everyone just commended on how pretty and beautiful she was as the days and weeks went on. I started noticing my daughter head I assume that some babies just had add looking heads, I asked my mom is this normal she said yes and for me not to worry at three weeks old I started noticing that her headbands, and her hats did not fit her head I just thought my baby was going to have a big head I had no clue or instant that anything was wrong was her one month's checkup the nurse came in to and done her checkup weighted measuring her and measuring her head etc....

And then the pediatrician came in took a look at her and did the same as the nurse did weighting her measuring her checking her ears nose so then Doctor walked out of room came back in again and did the same thing again. So now, I started feeling some kind of was I started having pins and needles in my stomach and now my mind is rambling in my head like what's going on with my daughter I started to cry.

And I said Doctor is there something wrong with my daughter he stated memo she is just fine just a cold I will give her a prescription to clear up that cold later on when me and my mom got back home my daughter started running a high fever and temperature. My mom and I took my daughter back to the hospital in glade water to the emergency room and they got us in and took the information they needed and then took us back to the room.

They took her vital signs and took her temperature and ran all kind of test on her doctor stated she had a cold and said to me that I'm going to prescribe her some antibiotic prescription. The doctor stated it will help her with the fever she had me and my mom went and got the prescription filled and immediately stated giving her the antibodies started giving every three hours as recommended. Now within a few hours, she started feeling better and now she was back to her normal self like what babies throwing her bottle playing with her toys walking in her walker eating etc...

So now my mom and I was so happy, going on doing our daily thing we normally do everything was coming alone very fine. So I decided to stop cleaning and went in and started playing with my daughter, I got up to go make her some bottles of milk and I sat it on her walking she threw her toys down and I put two bottles on her walker. She knocked one down and picked up the other bottle and started drinking she was walking and drinking her milk, usually she would be walking kind of fast coming into the kitchen with me and my mom, so I looked at her movement.

She was moving slow I walked over to her and I bend down and I started to rub her legs she started screaming and crying she was in pain. I continue to rub her legs then she started moving back, she wanted to walk and play I let her so then she stopped turned around and looked at me sadly like she was telling me in her eyes that she was hurting, so I went over to her and she started a cough and it didn't seem like a normal cough so I picked her up went and changed her gave her some medicine and put her back in her walker. I turned around to go back in the kitchen to finished what I was doing as I turned back around to look at my daughter again her head went back and when she moved her head back up.

I notice that she had some kind of white milk stuff coming out

4

of her nose so I just thought I did not burp very well so I got her up and sat on the couch to make sure I burped her really good so I sat her on the floor and I started gathering up her toys to give them to her I'm monitoring her at the same time Lafreshia decided to pull up on her walker and all a sudden she let out a cry I have never ever heard of before I called my mom and I'm crying and I said mother what's wrong with her my mom said he is ok she being just sleepy.

I picked her up and that milky stuff started coming out of her nose it was not dripping it was pouring out of her nose every time she bent over crying it would literally pour just out of her left nose it was like it was uncontrollable again took her tempura and it was so high so we rushed her back to the hospital the hospital staff and the doctor blew us off even though I knew deeply down that something was wrong with my daughter it was her brain leaking cerebrospinal fluids flowing through two cracks in the back of her sphenoid's sinus it was a condition that could have killed her after doctor again prescribe her more medicine again got medicine filled and immediacy gave meds to my daughter Lafreshia slept to 6:30. She woke up, checked her temperature and it had ranged up to one hundred and three rushed her back to the hospital and the time we got in the nurse took her and checked her temp now it is at one hundred and five.

The doctor ran in the room and stated we have to get her fever down or she is going to die now I'm crying I said please don't let nothing happen to my daughter. The doctor said it up to your God I said what do you mean my God, I worship my almighty high he stated yeah right so I just looked at him I couldn't say nothing else.

I had to focus on my child so then the doctor looked at me and said I'm going to do everything I can to help you I didn't say a word he then started calling the staff, she was having seizures one behind another

5

so the doctor as me to remove all of her clothes except her diapers and I was just crying my mom came over and put her arm around me and said everything is going to be ok. I told her no it's not they are trying to hurt my daughter I know this and I see this with my own eyes so they got the fever down again and said go home and give her this medicine I told my mom they are not trying to help her now I'm just fifteen years old.

I don't know about a baby but I know when something is right and I know when something is wrong and not going right. We went and filled the medicine again and again got home cleaned her up gave her a sponge bath and gave medicine it was not a second her nose started running again. This time it was no help it was like rain it was just flooding out of her nose I started screaming again my mom jumped up and got a blanket and wrapped her in and we took off to the hospital again I ran in and told the nurse that it was happing all over again and its worse now my daughter has lost her eyesight I was screaming and the hospital was full of people and she went in and got the doctor and he came and said to me look take that girl to another hospital I cannot do nothing for her anymore we don't have the right equipment for her he stated I'm sorry it's nothing else I can do or provide for you it was another doctor next door.

He had a clinic he was working late so he came running over there and he said get her to the hospital like now she has twenty-four hours and I'm going to call to good shepherd do you know how to get there my mom said yes I do Sir and he said I know a doctor that can help her I'm going to call down there and I'm coming with you she has to have emergency do.

I need to call a balance mother said no if you can get the police to escort us down there the other doctor said I will they escorted us there the staff was all outside waiting for her they put her on the structure started taking her clothes off as they were wheeling her into rushed her into the emergency doctor said they needed to get blood and cat scan soon in about fourth five minutes the doctor came in he said hello Miss Brenda and Mrs. Earnestine. He said I'm doctor gave his name and he said how are you I replied not good I ask him doctor is my baby going to be ok he replied to me with a long pass he said if you could come with me I want to show you something and go over something with you and your mother he said I wasn't to show you your daughter cat scan and a numb feeling just went through my whole body it was like a whole lot of goose bumps I just remember walking into the room not knowing what I am going to do the next moment tears started flowing down my eyes I ask what is it doctor, why me? what did I do something wrong is it a crime to love my daughter I never stopped looking to the highest even though I'm going through this tears just started flowing down my eyes deep down in my body my spirt and soul I just wanted to scream and hollow I just couldn't I couldn't do nothing in the inside of my mind it was like it just shut off I couldn't do nothing I couldn't even talk to the doctor I was crying so much I just couldn't help it and trying to stay strong was so hard so how could I stay strong and how can I hold it together I had to go to the book of Jeremiah 17;14 heal me, Lord I will be healed; save me and I will be for you are praise.

The doctor said as scary as it looks it's not good I replied what am I'm supposed to do the doctor said it's nothing. I could at this point and for doctors we can only do so much the rest is in the almighty high in job 5: 18 for he crushes but also binds up; he strikes but his hands also heal the doctors walked crying my eyes out yet feeling so lonely and depressed and stressed out room soon as I walked in and out a few minutes the neurosurgeon came in with my daughter cat scan and informed my mom and I the size of her head and how large it was and how the fluids are not draining like it was supposed to. So therefore the doctors said he would have to have to put the shunt in her head he explains it is a medical device that relieve the pressure on the brain it's an implanting flexible plastic tubes that divert excess a ventricular shunt is a plastic tubes about one eight inch with a vale that control to flow the cerebral spinal fluids draining from the cavities ventricles of the brain the doctor said we had to do the surgery soon as possible my heart was like jumping into my throat choking as the staff was coming in to prep my daughter for her surgery.

I watched them roll her out into the operation room the fear echoes into my heartbeat in Unisom the scariest thing to me was the waiting for the outcome of my daughter three hour had went by it was a waiting game but the waiting didn't go by fast it was like the time was going by Real slow and slower finally someone came out and told my mom and I that everything is going. Very well someone will let your u know when your daughter gets out of surgery it will be another hour they told me instead of sitting you and your mom go and grab something to eat if your daughter gets out within the hour.

I will call you so we did we only sat for thirty minute so me and my mom rushed back up the waiting room and sat back and started to panic and fear rose quickly in my throat wondering if my daughter is ok I went to the front desk at the waiting room. I ask where is my daughter is she alright what is going on all of these question was to come up to rushing through my mind through my head like a freight train.

I just had to see if I can find someone that could track down someone at the hospital to put all of my fears tears to rest someone then phone me in the waiting room told me everything is ok and your daughter is on her way to recovery soon as they come out they will let you know when she is on her way to recovery soon as they come out they will let you know when she is situated and you can go up to her

8

room finally in about fifteen they called told me and my mom to come up to my daughter room we did when I got to my daughter's room it was so heartbreaking that is was hard to see my daughter like this she was hooked up to all of tubes everywhere from the top of her head to the bottom of her feet. I was so scared to even touch her I just don't want my daughter to being in pain looking at my daughter gradually trying to opening her tiny eyes me and my mom's started reaching for her I could not even pick her up for crying so much it was just heartbroken to me just looking at her with so many tubes my mom reached in the bed and picked her up and turned to me and said she is going to be just fine come on and sit down and I will put her in your arms.

I just sat and cried and my baby Lafreshia just looked up at me with her tiny eyes l just knew that it was going to be a journey for me and my family this journey had just began with her challenges for her in Colossians 1:17 :19 and he is before all things by him all things consist and he is the head of the body who is the beginning the firstborn from the dead; that all thing might have the preeminence verse 19 for it please the father that in him should at fullness dwell; and Hebrews 12;1;3 therefore, since we are surrounded by such a great cloud of witness let us throw off everything that hinder that so easily entangles and let us run with the perseverance the race marked out for us fixing our eyes on the mighty high, the pioneers are perfected of faith for the joy set before him the endured the cross scorning its shame, and sat down at the right of the throne of the almighty. consider him who endured such opposition from sinners so that you will not glow weary and lost heart?

This journey has been very touching and horrible there was no way that I would have to go through this however it and it was a struggle and a battle for my daughter Lafreshia after everything has been said and done doctors said that my daughter skull was very low it is a chance or no chance she would walk or talk I didn't know how this would play out it was and it is a risk taker it was a success. I was so amazing at my daughter to recover when I see her restless eyes she had a vacant star of death the swelling of her head and how her head had grown and how her head had fever and it was very much hot just like fire shutting up in her body it was something how I had to watch her head swell like a balloon that was about to burst and looking at her head three time larger than a twin thin body as my daughter suffering from the hydrocephalus a condition in which excess cerebral fluids that binds up in her head and causing immense pressure and pain that referred to water on the brain this condition that has been described like a plumbing problem the fluids oh her brain that produce and it couldn't have absorbed normal and it started pooling in my daughter head it could have shut her eyes at the age of eight months in john 14:27 peace I leave you; not as the world give to you, let not your heart be troubled nor let it be afraid god had her shaft and God would be the one to pull my daughter.

Through I looked for doctors to help her and all the time God was working me as a mother I would have never known or even thought it would have been my daughter I had to look at things in a positive way it was so hard it was hard to even deal with this looking and watching my child go through such a bad situation you know it let all the possibilities swallowed me whole for the next six months she had unallied development delays associated such as taking longer than an average to sit or crawl while her difficulties she would catch up with therapy during January 1989 Lafreshia began showing sign of her first shunt malfunction such as sleepiness and nausea took her back to the hospital the CT scan showed and revealed that shunt had tissue impairing the flow of the fluids another surgery had to be done right away as her brain started showing sign of stress this second time my sweet baby had endured life surgery and yet she was wheel out of surgery and thinking

10

she was getting better my mom and myself had to stay in the hospital for three more weeks of February 18 1988 my daughter was released to go home.

I was so happy we finally made it home and unpacked it was still daylight it was good day so I decided to go outside with my daughter and put her in her swing smiling at my daughter that had overcame and unpacked it was still daylight it was a good day so I decided to go outside with my daughter and put her in her swing smiling at my daughter that she had overcame the hardest thing in her life and now living with hydrocephalus and now she will have to live for the rest of her life as I look back and as I'm thanking god for the shunt stopped the blockage of the water in her brain today my daughter has been through fifteen years without the complication of her shunt seizures she continues to take her medicine to ensure that it will continue to take control. over the past years Lafreshia has been an expert living with hydrocephalus and as I monitored my daughter I have found humor in what the condition that brings laugh and teasing Lafreshia short term memory loss is her side effect of hydrocephalus I have been told that that there is no recovery from the persistent vegetative state the condition of living like a vegetation in other words the edition without consciousness of like a vegetable in other words the existing without consciousness action.

The action the impression of being aware and the sentient of making random movements the opening their eyes and the response to communicate or demonstrate the awareness of the environment I understand the reality and the severely injures knowing that the defects as a mother I have to learned facing problems or life storms of any kind can be extremely difficult in the mist of heartache and the pain there is no hope and courage to go and move in with God help in Isaiah 41:10 so do not fear, for I am with you; do not fear, for I am with you with;

do not be dismayed, for I am your God. I will strengthen you and help you; I will uphold you with my righteous right hand. And the courage to go to your bible that is my resource and my strength that I received in psalm 107:19:21 then they cried to the lord in trouble, and saved them from distress he sent out his word and healed them; here sued them from the grave let them give thanks for the lord for his unfailing love and his wonderful deeds for mankind once again.

I see the smile of people asked how did I cope with all the things that your daughter went through I replied back and said for us its rally simple……. Just do what you can and just put everything else in god hands in psalms 147:3 he healed the broken heart and blinds up there wounds I am the optimism reader that has been extremely overwhelming a lot when going through the experience with my daughter it made me move forward and forgive and move to a better solution I was emotionally in a bad place when my daughter got sick in Isaiah 53:4:5 surely he took up our pain and bore our suffering, yet we considered him punished by god stricken by him, and affected. But he was pierced for our transgressions, he was crushed for our iniquities; the punishment that brought us to peace was on him, and by his wounds we are healed. I was so depleted anxious and I was giving my anxiety and feeling the attention for a while now I finally realize the feeling don't work like that I'm the type of mother with personality who tries to be optimistic and I made it through and I am able to move forward but here is the part I made it through by the grace of God.

In Jeremiah 17:14 it says heal me, lord and I will be healed, save me and I will be saved, for you are the one I praise. God cares through my daughter having water on the brain and all the damages and all the cries as a mother and the pain was very hard for daughter and myself this is a story lesson that god was preparing me for the whole time it was the waiting room for me not only just the waiting room, it was my life he was preparing me for something he had planned for me you know it's like this u know to me it was like going to the doctor appointment and you have already called or requested for an appointment the earlier you get in the quicker they can see you and you won't have to sit in the waiting room so as you sit you can count the fishes in the aquarium if so well you are on a time schedule right yes right but the entirely the doctors are discretion.

When you see him well I find the same truth with doctor God fills our lives with waiting in the waiting room when you are stuck in traffic stuck in groceries stores and you have to stand in line for a long period of time and it starts to cause delays and frustration well you still have to wait now you have planned the appointment and it should be over now you have to wait now you have to plan the appointment and it should be over now you know god has created each of us to do specific thing now if you read Ephesian 2:20. However, god has created each of us to do specific things however, god seldom put us immediately into places he ultimately desires us to serve there is a reason and god do reveals this part of his plan through his lives of those he chooses to lead; as a mother just like Noah he waited one hundred years for the flood and Abraham he waited twenty-five years and he was promise a son and joseph waited twenty-two years before his dream came true then there was Moses waited he was eighty years to liberate his people from Egypt it seems like the waiting get tough and it's for a reason it's on.

The reason why death comes and take to the garden of forever: we will never ever know why. I spent days and nights writing this manuscript its hope this story will help someone in dealing with death. It all started about a mother who was sitting by her child, holding her tears back as she was so sorrowful seeing her child's pale face, feeling her cold hands and hearing her shallow breath. The mother was so afraid that her daughter might die, and thought of it made her want to shout. This transition of a mother in front of a dying child is unbearable The mournful feeling of the mother her feel like she was in lucid dreaming like she was in another dimension. she felt her daughter`s spiritual presence, and she heard 3 knocks at the door, but she didn't know which door it was - the knocks echoed stronger so the mother stood up.

There she was someone standing in front of the door. It was a man, but the entity is stronger, she felt it. The eyes grew bigger seeing the man wrapped in all black. The mother was speechless as she looked down at her poor daughter whole breathing is fainting. She lifted her child finger, turned to the man and asked "What made you think I can't keep her? The good lord surely won't let you take her away from me". The old man nodded in such a strange way, which could have been a yes or a no. As she sat down with her dying daughter, her tears streamed down. She felt her daughter`s heavy head since her child has not slept well for several days. Feeling useless and a wreak mother, she asked herself "What shall I do?". Her child barely looked up to her and dozed back to sleep. She started shivering with coldness in her body and then asked the old man why do death comes to us.

The death of Lafreshia I couldn't forget that day which my whole life had changed never thought that I would expect another death my changed September 3,2018. I got up about 6am in which I always do going to check on my daughter straightening up my room like always doing my normal routine with my daughter she is watching me as I sing and tell her jokes we both were in high spirits, happy and carefree. Looking at Lafreshia it reminded me of April 19, 1987, a beautiful and a loving Lafreshia Lanet Green was born.

A blessing to her mother to her mother, Brenda Campbell;

Lafreshia also made the lives of people around her better and joyful. Her sibling: Telitha Rockwell, Korneshia Thomas, Shanquilla Green, were grateful to have known a very special person like Lafreshia. She always saw the beauty no matter how hard it was and no matter how hard the situation was. The mantra made her the best auntie to Arianna and Terrell and Ke`shawn. For the 30 years of her life were the best years of my daughter Lafreshia. She dominated her studies in Pittsburgh high school and joined a spiritual fraternity which brought her closer to God. however, that morning seemed gear and gloomy, I saw Lafreshia face, got up and placed her in her recliner and fixed her bed. I then turned around and walked out of her room and stood in the door facing the hallway- I looked back at her and suddenly saw her head fall backward. I immediately drooped everything I was holding and ran straight to her.

The adrenaline and the horrendous emotion ripped through me. I was trying to open her eyes but she wouldn't. she was unconscious but fainting breathing I was panicking while shouting her name out I ran to get my clothes on so I told a friend to grab the phone and call 911 I was holding my daughter then while screaming her name - in my head I was I was shouting "PLEASE BE ALRIGHT".my friend got in touch with 911 told them the situation we were then instructed to get her out of the chair and get her on to the floor to do CPR and chest compression until help got there we were asked about her breathing and we stated back that she is barely breathing. 911 kept on instructing us what to do while help is on its way to us.

I was hysterical already I could do nothing to my child moments later ambulance came right on in started working on my daughter taking her blood pressure putting oxygen on her eyes was check no dilation and that was not a good sign I just kept on holding her hands while repeating Lafreshia you're going to be ok you're going to be okay finally one of the guys said come get the mother so we can continually to work on her daughter. So one of the officers came and got me I just stood up and watched as they were helping my daughter it was so excruciating to see my daughter in such a situation the experience is unexplainable.

And life changing another took me into another room and starting asking question about my daughter her health and meds she was taking I finally answered all the question I just couldn't take my mind off my child then all of a suddenly one of the ambulance guys came I; while I'm still in tears I ask about my daughter he stated" for now let the machine do its job until we get to hospital we barely got a pulse the ambulance said "Mrs. Campbell; your daughter is brain dead." I was lost of words I just fell to the floor.

I couldn't stop thinking and crying about what had happened to my child the ambulance said we need to get her to the hospital; with a heavy heart I just looked as they carried her out the house they were doing everything for my daughter by the time they got her inside the ambulance it was raining heavily and I still don't know what to do and what to think. I was pale and discombobulated when I got to the hospital the nurses took my daughter while another nurse to me to come with her she put her arms around her and said everything is going to be okay Mrs. Campbell and she said continue to trust in the lord the almighty will put no more on you than you can bare.

I love my daughter just wanted her to be ok and to get through this so we can continue to have fun together doing things. The nurse said she will be just fine and you have to stay strong for your daughter and I said I have to be and she has to be ok even though the ambulance said she was already brain dead. I was told to stay in the lobby and someone will come back and forth and keep me updated and I did I waited 45 minutes wanting to know what is going on the doctor came out and I knew that was no good he introduced himself to me he asked me several questions if my daughter had fever or not I said "No I don't think so or maybe she had a little fever she was not hot though", "He stated she had fever for two days" the doctor responded I asked "How is that possible? I could tell she was eating and doing normal routines.... I said doctor just tell me is my Lafreshia going to be okay?

Now I still worried, it was a moment of silence made the atmosphere darker and everything even the movements of people and the sounds of people chatting seemed slow. Tears in my eyes drooped while waiting for the doctor`s response he put his head down and walked away I have to be honest Mrs. Campbell.... Your daughter did not make it", "What" .... You said she didn't make. The doctor continues but seemed inaudible to me I asked again so your telling me my daughter didn't make it because the fever went straight to her head which cause her to pass away "NOOOO it's not true! this is not possible! I begged to the doctor and held hands of the nurse, but they decided to give me space and went to inside a room. I was left in the lobby while crying very hard. there was a security officer, after his duty, who stopped and gave me his condolences. He had tears in his eyes and he told me it was going to be okay he stated to me. I don't know how it feel to lose a child he just looked and he didn't say another world just walked away in tears but in my mind it is not going to be okay I just lost my second child I'm crying and I'm just in shock it is just hurtful and it a lot of pain within me to lose another child. Never did I think that my darling Lafreshia is gone.

My beautiful daughter is gone forever and I never got to say goodbye or even hold her one more time. I just thought that something got to be wrong because everything seemed fast and unbelievable. The nurse came back and was looking for me since she needed to get more

17

information from me. The nurse said again "I'm so sorry Mrs. Campbell for your lost. Your beautiful daughter is now with the lord".

I said thank you much, the nurse stated again the lord will not put more on you than you can bear. I told the nurse that those words she had given me was encouraging words thank you the nurse said thank you Now I cannot think straight. I'm so broken hearted as the realization began to sink in- now all I wanted to do is go home. Within two hours, my next to eldest daughter came ask is her sister is okay. By the time the nurse came back she told my daughter that her sister did not make it now my other is crying what happened to my Lafreshia made me realize that I've been gradually losing my family. I lost my only son, I lost my husband I've lost my mother so now I just feel like job in the bible this is another worst day in my life.

Now leaving the hospital, I left with sadness and grief in my heart. I went home and coursed myself directly to my daughter room. Seeing all the things in her room made me think about all of the memories we had together. I started crying again knowing that I could never see me daughter again. I thought about the feeling of losing someone you love, my feeling of being alone; but I realized that I am not alone I have the lord with me in my spirit not having my daughter next to me makes me feel like screaming until I can't scream no more. I know that screaming wouldn't cease the pain I have but I just don't know what to do. for the next few days. I was trying to collect my thoughts Innocent dark figure 2021 me and it was a transition it was interesting to understand how and why death came in and - not only to me but also for those who has lost loved ones, especially a child with disability or a child that is brain dead or even a coma.

You to keep an eye on the order of the story to understand why death is death this is my enlightening explanation of death in my view, I

18

had looked death in different angles. A lot of time, if you can understand the way you see things, now before I can take you to see your child, you have to sing to me all the songs you sang to her. With triggered eyes she replied, why is this necessary? Are you telling me I have to sing every song in her life? Yes! I am fond of all of them, I always have been listening to you every day of your life. The night I came, I saw you cry while singing" the man reverted. "Okay, okay, okay... I will sing them, I will!" "I won't take NO as an answer" the man blackmailed. She asked for an assurance "So, once I sing them, could I have my child back?" the man nodded again which could have been a yes or a no "She finish singing with her eyes so red from the weeping and crying. "I did what you asked, now where is my child?" "She has not arrived yet. "The man grinned.

"what makes you think you will be able to find your daughter? Who would help you?" The good lord will help me! The lord is a merciful and you need to be too now!" she answered. Without hesitation, she asked the man where is my child is and where can she be found. But the man uttered the words, "I do not know", "you see? Many flowers and trees have withered, that's when I come in and "What is this?" The man stepped in, swooped in and took the child in just a blink of an eye. The next morning, she woke up and started preparing some things. She glazed at the clock in the corner, it was going haywire and looked heavy- it fell down on the floor and the silence was deafening. She stopped and rushed into the other side and yelling and calling for her child-she sat down and started hollered. Then the same man in black came and sat beside her- she stood up and asked, "Did you take my child? Have you been in my house?". The man answered earlier, "You must be fond of me?". She shouted out with pain and anger "Why?" The man said "I travel faster than the wind, and I would return nothing that I have taken." She felt they could wind slapped her face as the man flew away with her child.

Later on, that day, she couldn't stop crying and was still looking everywhere; hoping she can have her child back. The man came back and she asked. "Why are you doing thing to me? I only just want my child!" replant them. He continued" you know of course that each human being has its own life. Trees and flowers, each of them has a life. Human beings are like plants- yes! Flowers have heartbeats too." "Now, what will you give to me to? What else must do? The man asked. The mother just remained silence thinking that she has nothing to give anymore. The man continued, "I can only go with you until the end of the earth". She replied, "But I don't have any business there. And I have nothing else to give, I can only give you my white hair.

Besides, if this is really the thing you are asking me to do, then I wouldn't understand. If this has to do with me getting my child back so be it. I will gladly be part of it. The man smirked as they enter into a large greenhouse. She was unfamiliar of the place and sure it's somewhere she has not been before. She was unfamiliar of the place and she sure it's somewhere she has not been before. She feels a little concerned because the dark aura it gives to her. There was pretty palm, trees, plane and oak. There were plants that grew healthy while others grew sickly-where grass snacks laid. There were pretty palm trees, plane and oak. There was parsley and watering thyme. Every trees and flowers had their own name just like humans. All plants and trees had life like humans they all live here.

As she roamed around she then saw a large tree in a pot, repressed and looked like it was ready to burst- minutes after watching it, the tree opened and there she saw places that stood in a small drab. There were flowers in rich soil with moss around it. The feeling is beyond her comprehension, she didn't know why she is in a place like such, where her main goal was to find her way back, but the man came out from nowhere. "How have you been able to get here faster than me? The man asked her. "Because I am a mother! I am ready to move mountain just to find my daughter" she thought but didn't utter a word.

The man stretched out his long arms and hand towards the small fine flowers. She stood and looked at him and kept her hands tightly together. She was afraid of touching the petals, then the man blew on her hands and the mother felt colder that made her drop her weak hands. "You cannot do anything to me, only the lord can." The man replied, "I only do what the lord ask me to do. You see, I am just the gardener; I only plant them in- the-great paradise- in the unknown land. Now, how they grow there and what it is like, I cannot tell you that. The mother shouted to the top of her lungs and said "Give ME BACK MY CHILD!!!" Everything went back….

"What is happening to me? She asked herself. She cried out of death, she looked on the growing beautiful flowers. She felt the need to pull out those flowers for she is desperate. "Don't you touch those flowers, don't touch them! You are unhappy and now you want to make others mothers unhappy too?" the man shouted. The man wanted the mother to see what he got, but I didn't it was yours. Here, you can have it back. The mother whimpered and cried, she could utter no word. The man grabbed her hand and showed her to place flowers-gleaming flowers which indicates life. The man finds it necessary to give the names of the child the mother wanted to pick earlier. "This is what I thought I wanted, you liked to pull the flowers and destroy the destiny of the mothers. These flowers over there has been a blessing in the world and they're been another flowers of happiness. You may see some flowers show misery and sorrow, frightening as this may sound, but those flowers which showed darkness are the one I pick. Let me show you one flower and see how sad this may look."

The man showed her the dark flower… miserable… painful… the mother cried. "What you just saw was a flower I picked when you lost your child. It was her destiny that you saw. You saw your child`s future. "The man said. The mother begged for mercy, please I need to save the innocent child, I need to save my child from misery.

The man replied "your child has already been taken away. It has been taken to the kingdom. Her misery is long gone now, with the lord, your daughter will leave peacefully where negativity couldn't foster and life is forever happy". Together. I was walking all over the house trying to figure out what to do again. I'm left alone while trying to prepare for my daughter`s burial. I hoped it was just a dream, hoping that my child left the world. But the reality makes me wake up from that dream- my child is now Gone and that I shouldn't give myself false hopes. I contacted the funeral home in long view Texas at Stanmore. I did all the arrangement preparation for all the paperwork. While filling out the information in the sheet, I just didn't notice a tear fell down from my eyes. The preparation makes the pain more excruciating, I had to remember things about my daughter which makes it impossible for me to just remain ease, several days after, she was ready to be viewed at home.

Many family friends and neighbors came to give their condolences which somehow made the burden less heavy, some visitors schmoozed with me about the memories they had together with my daughter. I laughed and cried at the same time. During night time when people already left. I stayed up late to keep an eye on everything. I had to stay up late to welcome new family and friends who came in late as well. There was time I stayed up late, alone in the house. I want to look at my daughter but I just couldn't bring myself to look at her in the casket. It was so hard to look at my daughter in the casket. It was so hard to take my child in that coffin where I was wishing she was sleeping in her bed while sharing laughter. I was heartbroken, just seeing the casket turned my heart and my soul-part of me is gone.

I prayed for this child, and the lord lend her to me what I asked of him. So now I had to give her back because Lafreshia was not my child to start off with the lord lend her to me physically on this earth spiritually she had to be returned back to the almighty, 1 Samuel 1:27:28. I prayed for this child, and the lord had granted me what I had asked him. So now I give him to the lord. For his whole life he will be given over to the lord." and he worshiped the lord there. The day I wished the clock would move no more, October 6, 2018, came. I went to the grave site and saw everyone their; friends, family and neighbors. I got out of the car and looked up on the hill. From where I was standing, I could see the casket. It was white and gold trimming. As there was preparing, I still couldn't bring myself to look at my daughter.

So while the preacher was talking, I just kept on looking at her casket. Looking at it was like the lord had let me see through the casket I never seen my daughter during the awake so never could have guessed it. Telitha, next to the eldest daughter, asked me, "Mother what's wrong! I said I can see Lafreshia through this casket". My daughter Responded. Mother how I'm not certain "I told her She asked if I could describe her. I looked at the casket and then I turned to my daughter I said that her hair is in Shirley temples and she is wearing a brown goldish dress. My daughter Telitha said you are right mother you are definitely right!" she couldn't believe that I describe everything to her.

Before they could open the casket, I asked Mrs. Frankie if I could be dismissed she said yes! After the preacher finished with the ashes to ashes and dust to dust, I excused myself. As I started walking off I looked at the casket the whole time until they open it up it was so the family and friends could see her one more time. After everything was said and done, it was time to go back home. My grieving then started to roll into my life like a thick fog. "Brothers and sisters, we do not want you to be uninformed about those who sleep in death, so that you do not grieve like the rest of mankind, who has no hope. For that we believe that the Lord died and rose again, and so that we believe that the lord those who has fallen asleep in him.

According to the lord word, we reel you that we are still alive, who are left until the coming of the lord, will certainly not precede those who has fallen asleep. For the lord himself will come down from heaven with a loud command, with the voice and the trumpet call from the Lord, and the dead in the almighty will rise first. After that, we who are still alive and are left will be caught up together with them in the clouds to meet in the air. And so we will be with the lord forever, Thessalonians 4:13"17. My daughter will be with her loving late grandmother Earnestine green, her late brother Cadarrius Greenheart late stepfather Johnnie Campbell and her late Auntie Tonya Hannah, Christine Rollins, Uncle Billy Ray Green. My loved one has gone home. Sooner or later we all have to face death of a loved one. We meet this reality more than most because we belong to a bigger family the highest. The body of the most high blesses us many brothers and sisters, mother and father and all of our dear loved one whose spiritual bond with us will never be left mark 3:31:35.

We must have reckoned with death. Someday we will all comfort our own end, but along the way, we will witness our beloved friends and families leave. Death is a real enemy and frightening one. The last enemy to be destroyed, yet impossible to stop is death 1 Corinthians 15:26. I have watched my child pass away in front of me. Death is not ugly and it will always bring sorrow- nothing more than grief in your face before death. The lord himself wept over his own friend Lazarus. Johnn11:35, the lord has designed death to be unnatural to us-when I lost my child, I had to remember an important truth that me deal with my loss. Grief will be inevitable stroked me to the bottom of my soul. by the grace of our lord, sorrow does not have the triumph in my heart. The truth goes into me, as a mother, the faith that the almighty offered me was the insight.

In john 17:24 as I read the word on the close prayer, the reflection was very clear and it was my heart when my daughter died. I had to carefully consider my language. Father, I desire that also, whom you have given me; may be with me where I currently am and see the glory you have given me, because you loved me before the foundation of the world. As a man, the most high has certain desires on this earth and still has desired in heaven. The most high has to make known to the fathers, he speaks, as he often gives him. John 6:37, 39:10:29: 17:6 those whom the father has given to almighty should lay down his life. John 10: 11, almighty prays to his sheep in the high priestly prayer of John 17, as he continues to intercede for them till this very day- roman 8:34Lafreshia was unwanted by her father the unwanted child What does the almighty desire?

He desires that his people be with him. The almighty high is completely happy and satisfied as he reigns from heaven, but according to his prayer in john 17, he still has certain unfulfilled desires that people join him in the home of just pure happiness he has already prepared for them john 14:2:4. As I continue. We may lose but almighty high gains when my child in in the lord. I had to remember first and foremost that the father answered almighty prayer. The Lord is sovereign over our loved ones- life and death. And he was a purpose we would never understand. Deuteronomy 32:39 and James 4:14 but we cling to the truth that the almighty had prayed to his father to bring his people home. When my child died, father is granting to his son's request that the first prayed nearly two thousand years ago on the night before he gave his life for his people. I can say this much when I lost my daughter, the almighty gained a lot more than I had lost.

Now, looking at the eternal joy beyond the grave. The almighty knows he has a glory that is far beyond anything this world can offer. He knows that a true sight of him is worth more than a trillions worlds. He knows the sigh of his glory will leave no one unsatisfied. Alight is eager for happiness with him. We certainly taste many joys in this life, but nothing can compare to the delight on unhindered fellowship with almighty. We are designed for unspeakable joy in his presence. An answer to a prayer, when we lose a loved one to the lord, you have indeed lost at least for no. but that child has gained and so has almighty. Philippians 1:20:23 we may shed enough tears to fill the buckets but those streams enough tears running down our cheeks will listen with joy. When we realize that our loved ones' death is nothing less than to an answer to the alight prayer.

The death of my daughter, my loved on, in the lord may present on of the greased test of

faith. I can trust my loved that my loved one is better now off with the beloved. Will we have believed that the almighty is reaping the fruit of his work for sinners? If we do, then our grief, and almighty will turn our sorrow into great joy, john 16:20 "Precious in the sight of the lord in the death of his saints" psalm 116:15 and it can be for us too. We cling to the hope that death will never win 1 Corinthian 15:54:55. The almighty grieved himself so we will never have to endure hopeless grief in the face of death. The confession of a special need being a mother was undeniably hard!

As a mother, we can all agree that you are raising a little human from birth to adulthood, without instruction, and silently praying they turnout safe and happy. Now imagine if that tiny little human has been diagnosed with cerebral palsy and traumatic brain injury- the diagnosis could be physical, emotional or neurological. It could be obvious or maybe invisible to the outside world.it is scary, most especially for someone who is not doctor, therapist, and psychologist where there is no instruction or manual. It was just knowing in my gut that something was wrong. It was like feeling like a roller coaster, it was out of control. So being a mother, having no idea of what's going on, I entrusted to raise this tiny baby. I really did not want to believed that my daughter had been diagnosed with cerebral palsy and traumatic brain injury. I needed a lot to know and a lot of knowledge and understanding. As I turned to Lafreshia, I needed to vent my emotion help, thinking father should listen to me, expecting he knows I needed help.

The day my daughter died- breathe, grieve, and believe when my daughter died without being able to say goodbye. I have kept on wondering will I ever feel like this again? The grief I had was so painful so as my journey- a solitary one. But knowing and thinking about the truth calm me even in the state of grief. Psalm 46; 10 he says "be still and I know I am the almighty: I will be exalted in the earth". Stillness? Don't be afraid of it! I know when it is quite, my mind will be filled up with thoughts about the one I miss. I stayed quiet and that's when the almighty came in and erased unlikely memories. Being still, I was able to remind myself that although things was still chaotic, the almighty was still there and the almighty was still on time when you least expect it the almighty shows up- it was the almighty remaindering me to be faithful? I don't think I could handle what was before me, yet the almighty gave me strength, he enabled me to do what I thought was impossible. The almighty saw my weariness and knew exactly what he was doing on my journey.

I knew the almighty was right there with me that whole way in 1 peter 5:7, cast all of your anxiety on him because he cares for you. When I felt numb, that in 1 peter reminded me that he cared about me and which simply means that he cares about anything that I was concerned with. So when I was feeling anxious, I had to picture myself handling that care into the hands of the almighty. He was already aware every single time when my daughter died that I went through many feeling -being overwhelmed is one of them. I started to worry that I would not be able to make it. The lord knew how I was feeling inside and he is the only one who knows

who and what matters to me. The lord made my daughter back to him because he cares not to hurt me but relieve me of the tears. Psalm 56:8 record my misery; list my tears on your scroll-are they not in your record the lord seeing my tears as something valuable and remember also that almighty wept. Almighty was close enough to gather all of my tears and the lord also kept track of them. He valued every tear even the one slid down my check and not one my tears were lost with the lord. When I was giving, some people cried out for me, some people didn't and then there was people that hurt me. I approached a couple of woman and one of the ladies told me, "Your words really touched in a deep way". She stated to me that she was sorry for me and one lady said, I was touched as well. I might be crying on the way home". I cried out after I spoke with those woman, those small gestures stirred me up and my heart was like a wave of tears that washed over me- I just to let them come.

I finally realized that those tears I had was my healing tears and trying not cry was a delay of my grieving process. Proverbs 3:5-6, trust in the lord with all of your heart and lean not on your own understanding; in all your ways, submit to him and make it without my child. I kept trying to understanding but I could not make any sense of it. The lord is willing to direct me if I ask him. So that day when my daughter died, I was scared; but know this, the lord was there was there for me that whole time- he was waiting to lead me. The only thing I had to do was to reach out and just take the lord stretched hand. I had to receive the guidance, strength and the encouragement with the passage of death and learning how to cope with the topic such as loss, grief, and heaven.

I guess I would never be able to understand the gaping hole of loss that I fee, but I know one thing, all of the lord word was able to bring explainable peace and all of his scriptures were allowed to enter my earth and mind no matter what the stages of grief I will be. The lord was there the whole time beside me, walking and holding my hand like everyone else. He did not push me to move fast but rather guided me and gave me the strength for each of my steps. Psalm 116:14 says I was fulfilling my vows to the lord in the presence of all his people. John 11:25-26, the lord said to her, I am the resurrection and the life. The one who believe in me will live even though they die; revelation 14:13 says" then I heard a voice from heaven say, "write this; blessed are the dead who in the lord from now on "yes", says the spirit, "they will rest from their labor, for their deeds will follow them. "I have been thinking about those verses and didn't realize I was doing it.

Through there were times that people tell me that they honored me, it was not their child! It was not their daughter who did not make it. Almost all people tell me that it hurts their hearts, but in reality, I didn't know what to say. I lost my child and I just want them to know that I don't know what to respond and I just don't understand people. I remained quite as I heart time and time again because it fills me with deep and heavy sadness. I just wished my daughter`s heart had not stopped and I just wished everything was different and back to normal. I just wished I could have saved her. In Psalm 34:18 the old is near to the broken hearted and saves their crushed spirits.

For the love of my daughter, the day that she died was like the twilight of my grief. It was like I was missing all of the pieces of my heart- as I wrote this manuscript for my daughter, each note that I carried was like a different note, on September 3, 2018 when my daughter died, she was the brightest light that I have ever seen. But now that light dimmed with the passing of her death. psalm 147.3, he heals the broken hearted and binds up their wounds. I know that this would continue after her death, and I became well acquainted with anger, grief and fear. During the tumultuous time, through my daughter death, I came to know my strength, faith. The angel taught me to love and appreciate life. Through my daughter, I was shown how it was possible to go on even after the world knocked me to my knees and during times of feeling helpless and defeated, Matthew 5:4 blessed are those who mourn for they shall be confine. My darling Lafreshia was a fighter! She came into this world very fragile, but she was determined. My daughter proved so many people wrong in her short time on this earth. She taught me how to love and appreciate life through the way she found joy in the simplest of the things I would never thought in a million years that I would lose my daughter in such a way, nor the losing way in anyway.

I was just not ready for this. It was like a death for me as well, but it was catalyst for an immense change. I was forced to be stronger and I had to come face to face with my greatest fear of losing my child. At this time, I had no idea of the blessing that I received as I walked through I what I could say hell. I had to remember and reminded of the wellspring of strength beneath the surface. The fog of my devastation intensified the shift in the core my being. My journey to uncover my strength came as I sat beside my daughter, knowing in my heart that my daughter was fading, I had to promise that I would go on living in her honor and that I would carry on my daughter`s legacy of love even though my life was ripped off. I was left staring into abyss of uncertainty. I found comfort in knowing that my daughter is watching me from the other side and because I can still feel her presence.

As I lay awake in bed, I try to remember to let go and focus in telling the stories because it is very important to me and important to others. I want to let them know that they can keep on moving forward even after a devastating loss. I know with my heart that I owe it to my daughter to bring love to those who hurt to always remember that no matter how long or short life is, we should not give in, in Corinthian 4:16:18, we do not lose heart through our other self is wasting away, our inner self is being renewed day by day. For this light momentary affliction is prepared for us an eternal weight of glory beyond all comparison. As we look not to the things that are seen, but to the things that are unseen. For the things that are seen are transient, but the things that are unseen is eternal psalm 46:1.

I'm sorry that my daughter died I had four girls, now I am a mother of three. One of my daughter died and I saw the look on the look and the changes in the three daughters faces. My daughters did not realize that I could see the pain in them. Darning the twirling pain, my daughter Lafreshia was the source of me immeasurable strength. She was my joy, my deepest love and the apple of my eye. Lafreshia, was my first born. She was my princess! It was no surprise of that love I had for her the day that I lost her, it was no surprising of that love that I had for her. I lost her, it was long and surrounding emptiness, sadness, numbness and anger. The look of discomfort, unsure of how I am going to take this. When my daughter died, her eyes looked so heavy and I could just hear the deep breathing of her silence. I find myself saying sorry and look upset when someone called her name.

The death of my Lafreshia caused me to cry and seek help. I just don't understand the loss of my child. I just remained quiet because of the fear to be different for not being so quickly in coping up the way I am meant to talk to. I talk about my daughter but the question stills remain in my head, should I move on? How am I supposed to forget her? I watch as the children move from one school to another and having to school holidays. Me living with adult's children have grown up but I feel so sad one is not here with me she is gone on. As I hear time and remembering the wonderful work of abundant life has provided for her she had the best care for her it fills me with deep and heavy sadness- I just wished her heart had not stopped! I just wished everything was so different. I just wished I could have done more to save her.

Revelation 21;4 he will wipe every tear from our eyes. There will be no more death or mourning or crying or pain, for the old order of things has passed away. This is not all, one-day will come where our tears will be wiped away. Our pain will be completely gone. There will be so more sorrow, no more goodbyes. The lord will put death to death. I know it is hard to imagine, but isn't it's also wonderful? I mean, we will be reunited with those we had to say goodbye to. No more diseases that came along and robbed us from those we loved. Being a special need mother was very hard and it was just pure hard work.

From sensory therapy, getting new diagnoses, strike routines dealing with the meltdown, there was a lot going on and it was very difficult. It was very sad and very painful struggling while watching your child your child wheelchair bound and bed from day in and day out. I know that the lord wanted me to come to him no matter what good or bad when we are thankful, in trouble, devastated those times when I was upset, I had to turn to my bible to help me get through it,

32

and the bible brought me my peace, serenity, joy happiness and the bible calmed me the bible helped me get through and get passed in psalm 139:12 I praise your because I am fearfully and wonderful made; your works are wonderful- I know that full well. This verse gave me such encouragement when I was struggling with my issues losing my child. The lord made me know the struggle I would face. The lord designed and created me exactly he knew. Preface Psalm 139:16 for you formed my inwards parts; you knitted me together in my mother`s.

I praised you, for I am fearfully and wonderfully made. Wonderful are the works; my soul knows it very well. My form was not hidden from you when I was being made in secret- intricately woven in the depths of earth. Your eyes saw my informed substance. In your book were written, every one of them, the days were formed from me, yet there was none of them. What I loved: that lord creates all life Purposefully and that life began in the Womb. In 1987; my eight-month old daughter, Lafreshia, suffered brain injury. I believed that was manmade injury of the doctor who delivers her. This story talks about how my daughter is an inspiration to me and hopefully to others? How she fought and how, as a woman and a mother, was told that her daughter had no hope-no chance of living.

Being the mother of my daughter Lafreshia, I would like to shed some light on my emotion and how I learned that my daughter was hurt by a man and how I came to forgive. In Matthew 9:12:13 the lord heard this, he said "it is not those who are healthy who need a physician, but those who are sick but go learn what this mean. The worst lead me to read psalm 139, with promises that the lord was watching my daughter. In James 5:15, often to the lord; that verse says "and prayer offered in faith will make the sick person well. The lord will raise them up. Also in roman 8:28 ask the lord to work the entire situation for the good. The pregnancy and birth Jeremiah 1:5, before I formed thee in belly, I knew thee. And before thou calmest forth out of the womb, I sanctified thee. Pregnancy is indeed a beautiful and a magical miracle. When you leave the hospital with a glow, not so much with wounds it is evident all the years I saw pregnancy woman's out from the doctors' appointments. For the past years, I've read thousands of birth stories, I won't say that I've seen a lot, reading have taught me a lot. There for me were some important things: for me, no matter how well as mother's plan, if something doesn't go well as planned, we hope and think about that certain experience and wonder how we could make things go differently.

The day I went into labor, I had a major- bust of energy- I heard this from so many women including my mom, during her pregnancies. It was a fine day, I woke up in the morning, feeling antsy and distracted. Despite having things to do after breakfast, I went walking. The weather was warm and t was gorgeous which is actually good for me. After the walk, I went home and started to feel sick and tired. I told my mom about it and she said she was going to take me to the hospital. We got there and found out that I was pregnant and I was in my 1st trimester already. From day one of realizing my pregnancy, I was blessed. after going back and forth to the doctor, it was the time for me to have an ultrasound. I heard the sound of my baby for the first time which made me very happy! As the days and weeks went by, I started having symptoms: morning sickness, I felt an incredible bond with my baby. At 11 weeks, I had lots of crying and praising. In Samuel 1:27, I prayed for this child and I asked the lord to grant me. I asked him in verse 28, therefore, the lord had lent me my child.

During my second trimester, my belly had grown quicker and it was obvious that I was three months pregnant. It was time for me to go back to the clinic for my routine. Again, I had another checks up to make sure everything was fine. The baby is growing, on time in the inside of me, all praises to the highest, everything was fine, my rapidly expanding abdomen, me pregnancy was rambunctious, was starting to flutter with lots of kicks at sixteen weeks. I started to feel like tips poking me in the inside- what an experience! I felt completely in love with this little, tiny baby attached to me and utterly dependent on me. At seventeen weeks, I was scared of the feeling. I felt my belly get hard and soft. I started to freak out and thoughts started going through my head. Thank the lord and my mother whom I could ask what was going on whether or not everything is okay. She would put her hand on my belly and that baby would calm down. She said that the is okay she just kicking. I sighted as a sign of relief. But my mom asked if I would go to the hospital, if that would make me feel better, I said yes! My mother took me to the hospital as I laid on the table, while the nurse did an ultrasound we`re seen everything that the baby was doing good. She is indeed fine! All those kicking, my baby was doing learning back, putting her hands behind her tiny head and she would cross them she was just relaxing in the womb. Not only did I see my healthy baby move around, my baby move was never sluggish. She would push so hard where I couldn't distinctively make out a hand or a foot. I didn't know if my daughter was just testing the strength of her muscles, but she would hold for thirty seconds, so then she would kick so hard I would have my abs and lean back in my chair.

The nine-month pregnancy, every minute, was about my baby eating, breathing, sleeping, living, etc... it was all for her in my late pregnancy. Everything happened as it should be: my hip bone softens, I had stretched marks, I slept for nine hours, walked daily and could hear my daughter heartbeat. Time came when it is really happening, I was rushed back to the hospital since I was having labor pains- I was blissful. Nurses put me in a room and had me to put on a gown on to cover me up. Okay they have started hooking me up to monitors while the contraction had started. Every twenty minutes trying to see how far I had dilated. It was getting close, I'm getting annoyed and frustrated and angry. I was also crying because I was hurting and in so much pain. My back was hurting me so bad, I started to push the nurse and pushing the bottom. The other nurse came in with the doctor. They started rolling me into the labor room and the only thing I see was the ceiling. after pulling down two reveling huge spots lights, a mirror, a tray of surgical interments; finally, I had my daughter. The feeling was amazing with the most intense wave of emotion washed over me. As I simultaneously felt the most incredible love the strongest protection urge I had ever experienced. I can only compare my feeling at this time to a lion towards her cubs. There was something so indescribable about seeing a life-a new born. I was speechless as I glazed and hold her tiny hands. Through nothing else but just the overwhelming emotional experience after enduring birth, giving life to someone knowing that it was a challenge. Birth is just the simplest and the most beautiful things come to parenting. Clearer to me, this is a life experience with the passing of everyday. I had increasing peace and nothing could bother me, most of the time, I just feel blessed. I remember the desperation I felt, and realize that the lord delivered me and I was living his plan. For me, I was becoming a mother of life inside me. Throughout my whole pregnancy. The lord guided me to read the old testament to learn about the characters, as I read, I cheered on Moses, Joshua, Elijah, and David. I also had to learn more about the lord because he had his hands around me the whole time.

I never realized how exciting the bible is where at an early age the lord works in amazing miracles and how marvelous he created a day of life inside of me. While continuing reading, I made it to the end of jobs story where the lord allows Satan to kill all of jobs children and steal his worldly possession. In one swoop through multiple chapter a day, I was hoping to finish without dwelling so much on sadness. I finishing reading psalms by the time my daughter was born. I only made it to the chapter right before the lord spoke to job. John 9:2:3 "his disciples asked, who sinned, this man or his parents, that he was born blind? Neither the first diagnosis, it can be really difficult not to blame yourself. What did I do wrong? In my parenting that have caused this to my child? This was the question I kept on asking myself. I had to look at me. I had to look at me daughter`s picture and tell myself," I did nothing wrong!"

I know that the lord designed my child exactly as she is. My child had a purpose and I pray that the work of the lord will display in our children every day. Exodus 4:11 "the lord said to him "who gave human being their mouth? Who make them deaf or mute? Who give them sight to make them blind? It is I the lord? With a special need child, it can be very difficult to try to find an answer to the question: did I do something wrong during the pregnancy? Should I have done something differently when my daughter was born? I had to trust what the lord had designed; this is the lord specialty. The bible reminded that the lord is in control, and I had to trust and I had to lean on the lord and not lean to my own understanding. This had put my fears to rest, for a while. My perseverance suffering, my theme today is suffering joy perseverance and hope in suffering sadly with disappointments loneliness and sadness is suffering because the lord had to build me endurance in roman 1:2.

Paul declares that we need the gospel because of sin in Roman 3:4. Paul presented the content of the gospel: the lord acted to present the collision when I found myself in deep troubles when I found myself bruised. As a mother with a sick child the excruciating pain Lafreshia was my little girl can you just imagine that I carried her in my womb for nine moths nursed her fed her watched her grow but nothing like this before my daughter has lost the ability to all things like function independent on her own can any mother or events parents can image and how it felt to see their child bed written or even wheelchair bound and suffering with seizures day in and day out today my key passage as Paul explain how suffering produces hope he says we also rejoice in our own suffering because we know that suffering produces perseverance's character and character hope verse 3:4 john I have no greater joy than to hear his children are walking in the truth Paul explain we actually rejoice in our own suffering not because we like pain but because we know that the lord is using our suffering to flow of chart like the beginning the suffering that I suffered with my trials and building my trust with the lord the more suffering I went through was to build me for the trails in later life I've learned through this journey is when bad thing happened the lord has a way of using my hard times to bring beauty out of ashes he taught me to be tough through my circumstances I was willing to learn James 12:4 says consider it pure my brother whenever you face trials of many kinds because you know the testing of your faith developing perseverance.

Perseverance must finish its work so that you may be mature and complete not lacking anything I know that my life was not perfect it was not perfect when I was going through the illness of my daughter when I read the book of James knew that everyone who read his word would have suffering at some point in their life and he knew that the lord would uses these trials to teach us James wasn't necessary saying to take joy and pain itself James was adverting us to find joy in the result of pain in roman 5:3:4 only so but we also glory in our suffering because we had that suffering the year that my daughter suffered with water on the brain Isaiah 43:2 when you pass through the waters I will be with you and when you pass through the rivers they will not sweep over you when you walk through the fire you will not be burned the flames will not set a blaze. What happen when your child is bran dead? When someone is brain dead it means that the brain is no longer working in any capacity and will never again other organs such as the heart kidneys or liver can work for a short time if the breathing machine is left in place when the brain death is declared it means the person is dead when our loved ones are brain dead what do it mean it means that the brain is no longer working and capacity will never again that is the hard part that was for me as a mother the other part as I stated before will still work for a very short time if the breathing machine is still left in place so if the brain is dead it is declared it means that, that person has died. Can a child or an adult recover from brain dead? No that person who is brain dead is legally confirmed as dead they have no chance of recovery because the body is unable to survive without the artificial life support the things that looked for when my daughter was brain was her pupils did not respond my daughter shows no reaction to pain my daughter did not blink when light hit the surface her eyes did not move when the head moved.

The parent of my 30-year daughter it was outraged at the hospital then withdrew life support from my daughter whose heart lung function stopped moments later but the hospital officials said that to continue the ventilator after the confirmation of brain dead would be unethical arguing in essence that my daughter is brain dead already as question raises with the staff when is someone really brain dead and who gets to say so to raise eyebrows death doe sent always align neatly with the layperson's understanding of it especially that of grieving parents it's always been very difficult because the technology allows the brain dead body to be warm and perfused and to have a beating heart as another of a brain dead child it is and it is difficult.

I also had those thoughts as well how is me child brain dead it is and it was hard as a mother it was so hard to fight a battle to stop hospital from taking my daughter off from life support I realize when I went through this with my daughter that was a big turn and a big decision for me but I had to make that decision if I wanted my daughter to continue to suffer on the breathing or do I want to let her be free I wanted me daughter to be free and I didn't mean her to suffer no more at all I had to pray to the lord for my decision and the choice I had to do so I got the answer I wanted her brain to be release from that life support as a parent I was accustomed to making medical decision for my daughter her brain was different now if that child is comatose but not brain dead then yes it would be a different decision because that child is comatose so decision would be surgery would be done or whether the child was going to be put on a ventilator or a feeding tube was going to be put in but in those words you don't or you would not need someone consent or a family consent to declare that person is brain dead it is a judgement it is a medical judgement it is not a moral sort of judgement or quality life judgement my daughter suffered hydroscopic water on the brain at the age of eight months she survived until she was thirty years old in augh my daughter was declared brain dead the declared brain dead the examination found no sign of electrical impulses in her brain the staff declared her brain dead.

Overcoming the pain I've looked backed over my life and the damages that had been done to me and my daughter all the bad choices that is what made my daughter for example the enemy's doe sent show pain anguish in life I've experience pain my pain learned me how to feel better each and every day 2 Corinthian 4:17 this small and temporary troubles were suffered will bring us a tremendous and eternal glory much greater than trouble after living the pain, I've turned to the lord to help me rise above in the reading in my bible it always bring me back to reality. My deepest pain, it was my deepest pain, it was my result all of me darkest days my strength the lord had given me hope in job 6:10 this would be my comfort I would even exult in pain inspiring. I had not demised the almighty knows what he is doing he created me with capacity of my experience the overcoming of my pain and the overwhelming in my life it was my choice to overcome Jeremiah 17:14 heal me lord and I will be saved for you are the one I praise knowing when the lord gave me his word to help me soothe my spiritual aches but he also sends me his word to heal me all the vulnerable in my body was so painful the damages inside and out the betrayal rejection pain and suffering hurt it is a cut to my core and all the wounds were there for a very long time all I wanted to do was to be free like a flower like a bird flying in the tree I learned that the key that unlock that door is the understanding the pain was an enduring the life changing like water of a river the year's greatest pleasure that satisfaction came when I express myself all the years I've been through the pain and that impact I've overcame in roman 8:22 forward know the whole creation.

CHAPTER 2:

A MOTHER'S STORM

Let me start off by saying the lord have been moving when I started to move the lord started moving this was so true to me when the lord called for me for me to move. I had to move the lord showed up in a way the lord had been stirring my heart for sometimes I had to continue to pray to the lord I felt the need to move toward what? Psalm 18:31:32 for who is God, but the lord? And who is a rock expecting of? The God who is equipped me with the strength the alarm sound at any minute it's time to open my eyes I sit up and face another day things in my life couldn't get any worse all I could say is the lord got this under all the circumstance over whelmed me started taken toll on me I know the lord was with me through my unexpected journey with my daughter having hydrocephalus this was me bigger problem but nothing the lord couldn't fix I'm in desperation I prayed I cried to my Lord I know my lord was with me near I know he would get me through the lord wanted me to move me toward my journey as I stood helpless and watched my child go through what she was going through my first born all I could do is resurge my daughter that everything is going to be alright and give her lots of love and kisses every chance I could give her throughout the and night.

I stayed on my knees day in and day out praying for her my heart was so heavy just seeing my daughter, they gave me strength courage and my wisdom to be blessed as a mother and to make up for lacking of imperfect of a mother my worries of praying the spiritual implication all the transcendence the enduring pain that I had if I could trade places with me daughter I would for years I had to live I don't think I will not never ever forget that day that I almost lost her at that time and I would never ever let another doctor ignore my concern when I know something is wrong to this day. It still brings tears to my eyes how my lifetime and me experiences challenges communication and significance of my faith the lord had showed where whoever had been going through this journey faith the Lord let me write this story so others would understand this is a challenge it is a reason why I wanted to share this personal testimony at the time my daughter Lafreshia was going through her rough time my heart just felt like breaking into pieces everywhere it was like my heart was not there.

I've experience in my life time there is an old saying that the older purple use to say what does not kill you makes you stronger in 2 Corinthian 4:8:10 in every way were troubled but we aren't crushed by trouble were frustrated but we don't give up were persecuted but were not abandoned were captured but were not killed we always carry around the death of the lord in our bodies so that the life of the lord is also shown in our bodies when my life was inevitable there was many reasons why I had to go through hard ships dealing with my daughter I had to do be strong for the sake of the lord it was to strengthen me I know that the stars can't shine without darkness often times it demonstrate his faithfulness in providing me what I need to survive.

I know that the lord doesn't change pain in proverbs 24;10 if you faint in the day of trouble your strength is small knowing that my daughter having water on the brain it was the biggest change in my life a life journey I know that everything is for a reason and a season this was like a map of journey that I had to conquer it is the mountain and the trudging through my many valleys when I was approach my first mountain Lafreshia was eight months and she faced many hospitalization the struggles of her health this was the longest rough ride of my life as I thought of the worsts case scenarios running through my mind like a slow motion movie the question running through my head what's happening?

What do I do what do at this point whereas the relief what if my daughter doesn't make it what do I do as a mother you don't hear about your child it was not particular explanation for the devastation it was like a virus that had attacked my brain when I was going through this pain and endurance with me daughter in 1 Thessalonian 5;23 now may the lord of peace himself sanctify you completely and may your spirit soul and my body be kept sound and blameless for the coming off our lord nothing was easy for me I just had to take charge of my pain everything was like a project.

It was like life was hard just looking at my daughter and then listening to everybody telling me that my daughter wouldn't be able to function like a normal child I had to face and struggle with recurring that pain alone the path of my hidden feeling was like becoming a prisoner in my own mind I felt accompanies by my own tears my face expression had anger in me so many ways all I challenged was just unhealthy and unlucky an unlucky an unlucky disease of pain the reveling was too personalize vulnerability of me being quiet and being hidden in silence that was devastating experience I had to go through and had to experience the voice this trauma with my daughter that was kept closed in the back of my mind and not talking about it if I could go back to the night it happens to my daughter and fix it to give her a real chance to be a complete person but I can't it is just trauma for me the lord promises to bring me out and bring me through my storm in my life he reminded me his words was a great gain to face painful time difficult as it may be and yet I'm ever so aware of this as well it was easy to live through as well it was not easy to live through this I didn't ask for a hard time or a hard life and I know life was not going to be easy either I had to go through something nor did my daughter asks to suffer all I wanted was the storm to come and blow over our way I had to wade through the deep rivers of hurt rejections pain and I had to find my way out of darkness and the confusion but I know this was part of my life storms it was different this changed me and it did forever and the lord took what seem to be tragic and devastation to turn it around for the good it may not happen so quickly as I would like in job 23:10 he knows the way that I take when he has tested me.

I will come forth as gold tested tried and true Lord knows our way and we are passing through he reminds us that will come out to the other side changed for the batter stronger shinning beauty deepened from within the heartbreak and hurt and the feeling is like my heart is disintegrating into tiny pieces' lots of time my tears stream down my face and the weight of the heart was so heavy on my heart I am a better person having a relationship with the lord and it will remain with me no matter what the storms was life sent to me I know it would be a breaking point in Isaiah 43;1 when you go through the waters.

I will be with you and through the water they shall overwhelm you when you walk through fire you shall not burned and the flames shall not have consumed you these storms was always there the lord heard my cry he saw my pain more over my lord understood me as faithful to the lord for himself suffered he knows what is to suffer he is wonderfully able to help us Hebrews 2:17;18. Whatever we endure he cares is certain his love is in failing and his promises are secure also in Hebrews 13:5 he himself said I will never desert you nor will I forsake you I can say now that I know that I am not alone in the mist of unspeakable sorrow I know the lord was their beyond my understanding all I had to do is reach out to the lord when I was at my lowest with my daughter didn't expect her to make it and experience the storms and feeling like for me it was like my whole world had been turned down all alone in the mist the lord was telling me that I need to take back my life in psalm 139:7:10.

I can never be lost to your spirit I could never get away from the lord if I had to go to heaven you were there if had to go to that place of the dead you were there if I ride the morning wind to the farthest ocean you were even there lord you guided me your strength supported me in psalm David pictured the lord as great shepherd who provides and protects his sheep his children if you look at the verse 4 he says even though I walk through the shadow of death I will fear no evil for you are with me your rod and staff thy comfort me a shepherd uses his rod to protect his sheep by using his staff to guide them I can go on about my pain the lord knows in great details devastation that causes pain he understands the pain and sorrow the lord endures suffering experience pain of feeling abandon in Matthew 27: 46.

The Lord is always with you he knows that is always with you he knows that you are hurting he sees your pain he hears your cries your heart the cares deeply about us and attentive to every detail that burden us our heart in peter 5:7 say cast all of your anxieties on him he cares sometimes it may seem like life has been shaken to the core for the mountain may be removed the hills may shake no matter how bad things may seem the lord is in control nothing happen without his knowledge in Matthew 10:29:31 says not one sparrow what do the cost two for a penny can fall without your father more valuable to him than many sparrows what do they cost two for a penny can fall without your father more valuable to him than many sparrows if the lord eyes is on the sparrow he is most certainly watching you in the most of sadness and certainly his hands are there to guiding you his strength is there to support you. In proverbs 19:21 many are the plans in the mind of a man but it is the purpose of the lord that will stand as my daughter was placed back in the arms of the almighty high once again.

The day my daughter died- breathe, grieve, and believe. When my daughter died without being able to say goodbye. I have kept on wondering will I ever feel like this again? The grief I had was so painful so as my journey- a solitary one. But knowing and thinking about the truth calm me even in the state of grief. Psalm 46; 10; he says "be still and I know I am the almighty: I will be exalted in the earth". Stillness? Don't be afraid of it! I know when it is quite, my mind will be filled up with thoughts about the one I miss. I stayed quiet and that's when the almighty came in and erased unlikely memories.

Being still, I was able to remind myself that although things was still chaotic, the almighty was still there and the almighty was still on time when you least expect it the almighty shows up- it was the almighty reminding me to be faithful? I don't think I could handle what was before me, yet the almighty gave me strength, he enabled me to do what I thought was impossible. The almighty saw my weariness and knew exactly what he was doing on my journey. I knew the almighty was right there with me that whole way in 1 peter 5:7, cast all of your anxiety on him because he cares for you.

When I felt numb, that in 1 peter reminded me that he cared about me and which simply means that he cares about anything that I was concerned with. So when I was feeling anxious, I had to picture myself handling that care into the hands of the almighty. He was already aware every single time when my daughter died that I went through many feeling -being overwhelmed is one of them. I started to worry that I would not be able to make it. The lord knew how I was feeling inside and he is the only one who knows who and what matters to me. The lord made my daughter back to him because he cares not to hurt me but relieve me of the tears. Psalm 56:8 record my misery; list my tears on your scroll-are they not in your record the lord seeing my tears as something valuable and remember also that almighty wept. Almighty was close enough to gather all of my tears and the lord also kept track of them. He valued every tear even the one slid down my check and not one my tears were lost with the lord. When I was giving, some people cried out for me, some people didn't and then there was people that hurt me. I approached a couple of woman and one of the ladies told me, "Your words really touched in a deep way".

She stated to me that she was sorry for me and one lady said, I was touched as well. I might be crying on the way home". I cried out after I spoke with those woman, those small gestures stirred me up and my heart was like a wave of tears that washed over me- I just to let them come. I finally realized that those tears I had was my healing tears and trying not cry was a delay of me grieving process. Proverbs 3:5-6, trust in the lord with all of your heart and lean not on your own understanding; in all your ways, submit to him and make it without my child. I kept trying to understanding but I could not make any sense of it.

The lord is willing to direct me if I ask him. So that day when my daughter died, I was scared; but know this, the lord was there was there for me that whole time- he was waiting to lead me. The only thing I had to do was to reach out and just take the lord stretched hand. I had to receive the guidance, strength and the encouragement with the passage of death and learning how to cope with the topic such as loss, grief, and heaven. I guess I would never be able to understand the gaping hole of loss that I fee, but I know one thing, all of the lord word was able to bring explainable peace and all of his scriptures were allowed to enter my earth and mind no matter what the stages of grief I will be. The lord was there the whole time beside me, walking and holding my hand like everyone else.

He did not push me to move fast but rather guided me and gave me the strength for each of me steps. Psalm 116:14 says I was fulfilling my vows to the lord in the presence of all his people. John 11:25-26, the lord said to her, I am the resurrection and the life. The one who believe in me will live even though they die; revelation 14:13 says" then I heard a voice from heaven say, "write this; blessed are the dead who in the lord from now on "yes", says the spirit, "they will rest from their labor, for their deeds will follow them. "I have been thinking about those verses and didn't realize I was doing it. Through there were times that people tell me that they honored me, it was not their child! It was not their daughter who did not make it. Almost all people tell me that it hurts their hearts, but in reality, I didn't know what to say. I lost my child and I just want them to know that I don't know what to respond and I just don't understand people.

I remained quite as I heart time and time again because it fills me with deep and heavy sadness. I just wished my daughter`s heart had not stopped and I just wished everything was different and back to normal. I just wished I could have saved her. In psalm 34:18 the old is near to the broken hearted and saves their crushed spirits. For the love of my daughter, the day that she died was like the twilight of my grief.

It was like I was missing all of the pieces of my heart- as I wrote this manuscript for my daughter, each note that I carried was like a different note, on September 3, 2018 when my daughter died, she was the brightest light that I have ever seen. But now that light dimmed with the passing of her death. psalm 147.3, he heals the broken hearted and binds up their wounds. I know that this would continue after her death, and I became well acquainted with anger, grief and fear.

During the tumultuous time, through my daughter death, I came to know me strength, faith. The angel taught me to love and appreciate life. Through my daughter, I was shown how it was possible to go on even after the world knocked me to my knees and during times of feeling helpless and defeated, Mathew 5:4 blessed are those who mourn for they shall be confine. My darling Lafreshia was a fighter! She came into this world very fragile, but she was determined. My daughter proved so many people wrong in her short time on this earth. She taught me how to love and appreciate life through the way she found joy in the simplest of the things.

I would never have thought in a million years that I would lose my daughter in such a way, nor the losing way in anyway- I was just not ready for this. It was like a death for me as well, but it was catalyst for an immense change. I was forced to be stronger and I had to come face to face with my greatest fear of losing my child. At this time, I had no idea of the blessing that I received as I walked through I what I could say hell. I had to remember and reminded of the wellspring of strength beneath the surface. The fog of my devastation intensified the shift in the core my being. My journey to uncover my strength came as I sat beside my daughter, knowing in my heart that my daughter was fading, I had to promise that I would go on living in her honor and that I would carry on my daughter`s legacy of love even though my life was ripped off. I was left staring into abyss of uncertainty. I found comfort in knowing that my daughter is watching me from the other side and because I can still feel her presence. As I lay awake in bed, try to remember to let go and focus in telling the stories because it is very important to me and important to others. I want to let them know that they can keep on moving forward even after a devastating loss. I know with my heart that I owe it to my daughter to bring love to those who hurt to always remember that no matter how long or short life is, we should not give in.

In Corinthian 4:16:18, we do not lose heart through our other self is wasting away, our inner self is being renewed day by day. For this light momentary affliction is prepared for us an eternal weight of glory beyond all comparison. As we look not to the things that are seen, but to the things that are unseen. For the things that are seen are transient, but the things that are unseen is eternal psalm 46:1. I'm sorry that my daughter died I had four girls, now I am a mother of three. One of my daughter died and I saw the look on the look and the changes in the three daughters faces. My daughters did not realize that I could see the pain in them. Darning the twirling pain, my daughter Lafreshia was the source of me immeasurable strength. She was my joy, my deepest love and the apple of my eye. Lafreshia, was my first born. She was my princess! It was no surprise of that love I had for her. The day that I lost her, it was no surprising of that love that I had for her. I lost her, it was long and surrounding emptiness, sadness, numbness and anger. The look of discomfort, unsure of how I am going to take this.

When my daughter died, her eyes looked so heavy and I could just hear the deep breathing of her silence. I find myself saying sorry and look upset when someone called her name. The death of my Lafreshia caused me to cry and seek help. I just don't understand the loss of my child. I just remained quiet because of the fear to be different, for not being so quickly in coping up the way I am meant to talk to. I talk about my daughter but the question stills remain in my head, should I move on? How am I supposed to forget her? I watch as the children move from one school to another and having to school holidays. Me living adult's children have gowned up but I feel so sad one is not here with me she is gone on. As I hear time and remembering the wonderful work of abundant life has provided for her she had the best care for her it fills me with deep and heavy sadness.

I just wished her heart had not stopped! I just wished everything was so different. I just wished I could have done more to save her. Revelation 21;4 he will wipe every tear from our eyes. There will be no more death or mourning or crying or pain, for the old order of things has passed away. This is not all, one-day will come where our tears will be wiped away. Our pain will be completely gone. There will be so more sorrow, no more goodbyes. The lord will put death to death. I know it is hard to imagine, but isn't it's also wonderful? I mean, we will be reunited with those we had to say goodbye to. No more diseases that came along and robed us from those we loved. Being a special need mother was very hard and it was just pure hard work. From sensory therapy, getting new diagnoses, stick routines dealing with the meltdown, there was a lot going on and it was very difficult. It was very sad and very painful struggling while watching your child your child wheelchair bound and bed from day in and day out. I know that the lord wanted me to come to him no matter what good or bad when we are thankful, in trouble, devastated those times when I was upset, I had to turn to my bible to help me get through it, and the bible brought me my peace, serenity, joy happiness and the bible calmed me the bible helped me get through and get passed in psalm 139:12 I praise your because I am fearfully and wonderful made; your works are wonderful- I know that full well. This verse gave me such encouragement when I was struggling with my issues losing my child. The lord made me know the struggle I would face. The lord designed and created me exactly he knew. Preface Psalm 139:16 for you formed my inwards parts; you knitted me together in my mother`s.

I praised you, for I am fearfully and wonderfully made.

Wonderful are the works; my soul knows it very well. My form was not hidden from you when I was being made in secret- intricately woven in the depths of earth. Your eyes saw my informed substance. In your book were written, every one of them, the days were formed from me, yet there was one of them. A mother's storm let me start off by saying the lord have been moving when I started to move the lord started moving this was so true to me when the lord called for me for me to move I had to move the lord showed up in a way the lord had been stirring my heart for sometimes I had to continue to pray to the lord I felt the need to move toward what? Psalm 18:31:32 for who is god, but the lord? And who is a rock expecting of? The God who is equipped me with the strength the alarm sound at any minute it's time to open my eyes I sit up and face another day things in my life couldn't get any worse all I could say is the lord got this under all the circumstance over whelmed me started taken toll on me. I know the lord was with me through my unexpected journey with my daughter having hydrocephalus this was me bigger problem but nothing the lord couldn't fix I'm in desperation I prayed I cried to my lord I know my lord was with me near I know he would get me through the lord wanted me to move me toward my journey as I stood helpless and watched my child go through what she was going through my first born all I could do is resurrect my daughter that everything is going to be alright and give her lots of love and kisses every chance I could give her throughout the and night.

I stayed on my knees day in and day out praying for her my heart was so heavy just seeing my daughter, they gave me strength courage and my wisdom to be blessed as a mother and to make up for lacking of imperfect of a mother my worries of praying the spiritual implication all the transcendence the enduring pain that I had if I could trade places with me daughter I would for years I had to live I don't think I will not never ever forget that day that I almost lost her at that time and I would never

ever let another doctor ignore my concern when I know something is wrong to this day it still brings tears to my eyes how my lifetime and me experiences challenges communication and significance of my faith the lord had showed where whoever had been going through this journey faith the lord let me write this story so others would understand this is a challenge it is a reason why I wanted to share this personal testimony at the time my daughter Lafreshia was going through her rough time my heart just felt like breaking into pieces everywhere it was like my heart was not there I've experience in my life time there is an old saying that the older purple use to say what doesn't kill you makes you stronger in 2 Corinthians 4:8:10 in every way were troubled but we aren't crushed by trouble were frustrated but we don't give up were persecuted but were not abandoned were captured but were not killed we always carry around the death of the lord in our bodies so that the life of the lord is also shown in our bodies when my life was inevitable there was many reasons why I had to go through hard ships dealing with my daughter I had to do be stung for the sake of the lord it was to strengthen me.

I know that the stars can't shine without darkness often times it demonstrate his faithfulness in providing me what I need to survive I know that the lord doesn't change pain in proverbs 24;10 if you faint in the day of trouble your strength is small knowing that my daughter having water on the brain it was the biggest change in my life a life journey I know that everything is for a reason and a season this was like a map of journey that I had to conquer it is the mountain and the trudging through my many valleys when I was approach my first mountain Lafreshia was eight months and she faced many hospitalization the struggles of her health this was the longest rough ride of my life as I thought of the worsts case scenarios running through my mind like a slow motion movie the question running through my head what's happening? What do I do what do at this point where? is the relief what if my daughter doesn't make it what do I do as a mother you don't hear about your child it was not particular explanation for the devastation it was like a virus that had attacked my brain when I was going through this pain and endurance with me daughter in 1 Thessalonian 5;23.

Now may the lord of peace himself sanctify you completely and may your spirit soul and my body be kept sound and blameless for the coming off our lord nothing was easy for me I just had to take charge of my pain everything was like a project it was like life was hard just looking at my daughter and then listening to everybody telling me that my daughter wouldn't be able to function like a normal child I had to face and struggle with recurring that pain alone the path of my hidden feeling was like becoming a prisoner in my own mind I felt accompanies by my own tears my face expression had anger in me so many ways all.

I challenged was just unhealthy and unlucky an unlucky an unlucky disease of pain the reveling was too personalize vulnerability of me being quiet and being hidden in silence that was devastating experience. I had to go through and had to experience the voice this trauma with my daughter that was kept closed in the back of my mind and not talking about it if I could go back to the night it happens to my daughter and fix it to give her a real chance to be a complete person but I can't it is just trauma for me the lord promises to bring me out and bring me through my storm in my life he reminded me his words was a great gain to face painful time difficult as it may be and yet I'm ever so aware of this as well it was easy to live through as well it was not easy to live through this.

I didn't ask for a hard time or a hard life and I know life was not going to be easy either I had to go through something nor did my daughter asks to suffer all I wanted was the storm to come and blow over our way I had to wade through the deep rivers of hurt rejections pain and I had to find my way out of darkness and the confusion but I know this was part of my life storms it was different this changed me and it did forever and the lord took what seem to be tragic and devastation to turn it around for the good it may not happen so quickly as I would like in job 23:10. He knows the way that I take when he has tested me I will come forth as gold tested tried and true lord knows our way and we are passing through he reminds us that will come out to the other side changed for the batter stronger shinning beauty deepened from within the heartbreak and hurt and the feeling is like my heart is disintegrating into tiny pieces' lots of time my tears stream down my face and the weight of the heart was so heavy on my heart I am a better person having a relationship with the lord and it will remain with me no matter what the storms was life sent to me I know it would be a breaking point in Isaiah 43;1.

When you go through the waters I will be with you and through the water they shall overwhelm you when you walk through fire you shall not burned and the flames shall not have consumed you these storms was always there the lord heard my cry he saw my pain more over my lord understood me as faithful to the lord for himself suffered he knows what is to suffer he is wonderfully able to help us Hebrews 2:17;18 whatever we endure he cares is certain his love is in failing and his promises are secure also in Hebrews 13:5.

He himself said I will never desert you nor will I forsake you I can say now that I know that I am not alone in the mist of unspeakable sorrow I know the lord was their beyond my understanding all I had to do is reach out to the lord when I was at my lowest with my daughter didn't expect her to make it and experience the storms and feeling like for me it was like my whole world had been turned down all alone in the mist the lord was telling me that I need to take back my life in psalm

139:7:10 I can never be lost to your spirit.

I could never get away from the lord if I had to go to heaven you were there if I had to go to that place of the dead you were there if I ride the morning wind to the farthest ocean you were even there lord you guided me your strength supported me in psalm David pictured the lord as great shepherd who provides and protects his sheep his children if you look at the verse 4 he says even though I walk through the shadow of death I will fear no evil for you are with me your rod and staff thy comfort me a shepherd uses his rod to protect his sheep by using his staff to guide them I can go on about my pain the lord knows in great details devastation that causes pain he understands the pain and sorrow the lord endures suffering experience pain of feeling abandon in Matthew 27: 46. The lord is always with you he knows that is always with you he knows that you are hurting he sees your pain he hears your cries your heart the cares deeply about us and attentive to every detail that burden us our heart in peter 5:7 say cast all of your anxieties on him he cares sometimes it may seem like life has been shaken to the core for the mountain may be removed the hills may shake.

No matter how bad things may seem the lord is in control nothing happen without his knowledge in Matthew 10:29:31 says not one sparrow what do the cost two for a penny can fall without your father more valuable to him than many sparrows what do they cost two for a penny can fall without your father more valuable to him than many sparrows if the lord eyes is on the sparrow he is most certainly watching you in the most of sadness and certainly his hands are there to guiding you his strength is there to support you. In proverbs 19:21 many are the plans in the mind of a man but it is the purpose of the lord that will stand as my daughter was placed back in the arms of the almighty high once again What happen when your child is bran dead? When someone is brain dead it means that the brain is no longer working in any capacity?

And will never again other organs such as the heart kidneys or liver can work for a short time if the breathing machine is left in place when the brain death is declared it means the person is dead. When our loved ones are brain dead what do it mean it means that the brain is no longer working and capacity will never again that is the hard part that was for me as a mother the other part as I stated before will still work for a very short time if the breathing machine is still left in place so if the brain is dead it is declared it means that, that person has died. Can a child or an adult recover from brain dead?

No that person who is brain dead is legally confirmed as dead they have no chance of recovery because the body is unable to survive without the artificial life support the things that looked for when my daughter was brain was her pupils did not respond my daughter shows no reaction to pain my daughter did not blink when light hit the surface her eyes did not move when the head moved. The parent of my 30-year daughter it was outraged at the hospital the withdrew life support from my daughter whose heart lung function stopped moments later but the hospital officials said that to continue the ventilator after the confirmation of brain dead would be unethical arguing in essence that my daughter is brain dead already. As question raises with the staff when is someone really brain dead and who gets to say so to raise eyebrows death doesn't always align neatly with the layperson's understanding of it especially that of grieving parents.

It's always been very difficult because the technology allows the brain dead body to be warm and perfused and to have a beating heart as a mother of a brain dead child it is and it is difficult. I also had those thoughts as well how is me child brain dead it is and it was hard as a mother it was so hard to fight a battle to stop hospital from taking my

58

daughter off from life support. I realize when I went through this with me daughter that was a big turn and a big decision for me but I had to make that decision if I wanted my daughter to continue to suffer on the breathing or do I want to let her be free. I wanted my daughter to be free and I didn't mean her to suffer no more at all I had to pray to the lord for me decision and the choice I had to do so I got the answer I wanted her brain to be release from that life support as a parent. I was accustomed to making medical decision for my daughter her brain was different now if that child is comatose but not brain dead then yes it would be a different decision because that child is comatose so decision would be surgery would be done or whether the child was going to be put on a ventilator or a feeding tube was going to be put in but in those words you don't or you would not need someone consent or a family consent to declare that person is brain dead. It is a judgement it is a medical judgement it is not a moral sort of judgement or quality life judgement my daughter suffered hydroscopic water on the brain at the age of eight months she survived until she was thirty years old in August my daughter was declared brain dead the declared brain dead the examiner found no sign of electrical impulses in her brain the staff declared her brain dead. The confession of a special need being a mother was hard I think as a mother we can all agree in that you are raising a little human from birth to adulthood without an instruction and silently praying they turn out sane and happy now imagine if that tiny little human has been diagnosis with cerebral palsy and trauma brain injury the diagnosis could be physical emotional or neurological it could be obvious or maybe it's invisible to the outside world. Now that's scary. I am not a doctor therapist physiologist there is no instruction manual it was just knowing in my gut that something was wrong this that I was feeling was like a roller coaster it was out of control and just me being the mother that I am I had no idea what's going on but yet I entrusted to raise this tiny baby.

I really did not want to believe that my daughter had been diagnosis with cerebral palsy and diagnosis with trauma brain injury I needed a lot to know and a lot of knowledge I needed to vent and I needed understanding as I turned to Lafreshia father thinking he would listen to me knowing I needed the help the only thing he did was gave me the death ear he has no kind of conversation for me when it came down to his daughter he always had a strange look at me and at his daughter not even wanted to communicated with her the only that really came out of his mouth was judgmental words towards me. While words can never fully express how much someone means to us, language can still provide comfort, solace, hope, and even inspiration following the death of a loved one. Proverbs and folk sayings about death, grief, and mourning from a variety of cultural traditions can sometimes speak the words you are unable to express yourself.

Holding hands

There are a great variety of cultural traditions surrounding death, as well as different emotions and perspectives on what it means. From honoring a person who died to supporting the living, to adding a touch of humor, these time-honored proverbs reflect these vast differences.

Words of Inspiration After a Death

Proverbs and sayings may be helpful in many different ways after the loss of a loved one. They might comfort you as you are mourning alone. They may help you as you write a eulogy, or pen a condolence letter to a loved one. They can be particularly helpful when you are simply trying to find the right words, and need a little inspiration.

Sayings That Honor a Person Who Has Died

Everyone dies, but it can be particularly painful when a loved one who was particularly good to us dies.

Say not in grief he is no more, but live in thankfulness that he was.

Good men must die, but death cannot kill their names.

Proverbs That Remind Us That Our Loved Ones Live on Through Us

While your loved one has gone, their memory remains. And as much as that memory remains a part of you, it remains alive.

As long as we live, they too will live, for they are now a part of us, as

We remember them.

Only love gives us the taste of eternity.

The only truly dead are those who have been forgotten.

Proverbs That Express Grief in Those Who Remain

Grief is painful, and at times you may feel your heart is literally breaking. Viewing tears as cleansing, and receiving the sympathy of others, can be healing during this time.

What soap is for the body, tears are for the soul.

God is closest to those with broken hearts.

Sympathy is a little medicine to soothe the ache in another's heart.

Proverbs That View Death as a Normal Part of Life

Some cultures view death as a very normal part of life on a continuum., it's almost forgotten that everyone must someday die.

Life is not separate from death. It only looks that way.

Everything revolves around bread and death.

One is certain only of death.

There is no one who can jump so high as to escape death.

Who is old and doesn't believe it, will trip into his grave without seeing it.

All who have died are equal.

Death doesn't knock on the door.

Proverbs That Help in Letting Go

It was important to honor those who have gone before us, and it can be very hard to let go. Even though a loved one would wish us to move on and enjoy our lives, it's a difficult step to take. to me I had to remember that I had to grieve the loss of my loved one, but that grief become less acute in time. In fact, after a time, remembering my loved one may bring more comfort than pain.

All things grow with time -- except grief.

Who dies, dies, and who lives, lives.

Live your own life, for you will die your own death.

Proverbs That Remind Us to Live Our Lives Today

A death is a reminder to all of us that our lives are finite. Sometimes seeing death is a reminder to live today.

If you start thinking of death, you are no longer sure of life.

Everybody will undergo the sentence of the grave.

Death doesn't just look through the book of the old.

Proverbs About Death with a Touch of Humor

There is a time for everything. Humor is not the usual "go to" following a death but can be very helpful in the right setting. Sometimes a bit of humor can be a blessing during deep grief. At other times, it may help those who are coping with strained pre-death relationships.

Old age is not as honorable as death, but most people want it.

What you give for the cause of charity in health is gold; what you give in sickness is silver; what you give after death is lead.

Miscellaneous Death Proverbs

There are many death proverbs that wouldn't be appropriate for a memorial service but reflect on death in other ways.

The death of an elderly man is like a burning library.

The ugliest life is better than the nicest death.

The whole world is a dream, and death the interpreter.

There is a cure for everything except death.

Words for Coping with Death

Words in proverbs, and prose can often describe feelings you're unable to express alone. Poems about death and loss can add another dimension, and describe emotions more fully at times. Death and grief quotations may also capture what you are trying to express, whether it is silent as you go through your own grief, or as you write a eulogy.

A Word from Very well on Death Proverbs

If you've arrived here looking for proverbs about death, it's likely you are grieving. Whether the person you have lost was very close, or whether your relationship was strained or ended prior to death, your heart will be tender. There is a sense of loss no matter the type of relationship you had, and no matter how close you were.

Losing those very close to us is painful. But losing those more distant hurts deeply as well. Not only for the times together but for the memories which are inevitably stirred in your heart concerning previous losses. Losing someone very close to your heart is like losing a part of yourself. Yet losing someone who is not so near, someone you are estranged from, perhaps, is remarkably painful as well. In death, the door is closed against hope of something different in the future.

Grieving, give yourself time. Everyone grieves differently and for different periods of time. There isn't a right or wrong way to grieve, only the way that is right for you.

Death to Live a Meaningful Life

Man Walking on top of a mountain during sunset

Life is such a wonderful gift, it makes me humble every single time I stop and think about it. Death on the other hand is scary to think about. I still cannot fully comprehend it. Think about going to sleep and never waking up again. Step away from your laptop, cell phone, or computer and think about that for a minute or so. Go ahead, I'll wait.

Are you back? How weird is that to think about? What's that feeling like?

Thinking about death stretches and alters your perception. Accepting something you cannot change reduces suffering. It allows you to overcome fear and punch it right in the face. It also reveals the importance of love.

Many people don't realize, until it's too late, that cherishing your friends and family should be your number one priority. Yes, you hear it all the time and think it's cheesy, but before you leave you'll realize how important the people in your life really are

I believe that once you come face to face with death, you'll drop your silly ego and become much humbler than you currently are.

What boggles my mind, is that our society tends to sweep the topic of death under the carpet. They don't want to think about it now, and will worry about it later. Why!? I would argue it's one of the most important things to think about NOW.

I don't want to bring religion into this subject because logically speaking, there is no evidence for life after death. If there was, then we would all know by now and the "debate" about this subject wouldn't exist. I'm quite aware of the near death experience stories, but once again things get quite blurry once you "dive in" the details and try to critically make "sense" of it.

Now I don't want to sound like a downer, I personally stay optimistic about this sort of thing. After all, it's quite scary to imagine you never existing again and simply rotting in the ground. As I'm writing this, I feel goosebumps slowly creeping all over my body just from thinking about it. But this isn't a bad thing, in fact it's very inspiring.

How is it inspiring?

If you think about it, it makes you suddenly realize that a day will come when you will have to "check out." All of your money and material possessions will simply vanish. Sure, the people in your will might receive them, however you will no longer own them or really need them. While I cannot know for sure, the scariest part is that there is a chance of your memories and knowledge simply vanishing as well. This theory breaks my heart the most. It makes you ask the oldest question in the world, "What is the meaning for life?"

It's interesting to think that one day, out of nowhere, you came into existence. Was that by luck or purpose? Can you find an answer to that question? I don't think so.

For the first time ever you saw light after being in the darkness. You came here with free will not knowing what to do or what path to follow. It's kind of like playing a first person video game, without having an option to respawn...

Thinking about death allows you to figure out what your priorities in life should be. Everybody wants to die in peace without any regrets. You must figure out what you want to accomplish and create multiple goals for yourself.

You can achieve anything and be anybody you want to be. Other people on Earth are humans just like you. They are flesh and bones, just like you. You have the ability to do anything that they do. The only limit is the one you set yourself.

I'm always baffled by how people constantly devalue their own life and create silly excuses for themselves. If you're one of those people, you need to get a hold of yourself and make the best out of the cards you've been dealt.

Most older people usually say "You're far too young to be thinking about death." I never understood that. It's basically the worst kind of procrastinating one could do. I believe that you never really live, until you overcome death. Once you face it and come at peace with it, you can actually start living your life to the fullest.

You came into this world alone and you will leave this world alone. Don't be distracted from your inevitable demise. Use it to your advantage and live the life you want to live. If you do that, I guarantee that right before you die you will be happy that you listened to this advice. You will smile about it, rather than be saddened by treacherous regret.

Even if we never physically meet, I hope my message will help you live a remarkable life. I hope you'll accomplish everything you've ever dreamed of. I hope you'll succeed in every single thing you try.

A Compilation of grief to Uplift Your Sadness

"No one ever told me that grief felt so like fear. I am not afraid, but the sensation is like being afraid. The same fluttering in the stomach, the same restlessness, the yawning. I keep on swallowing. At other times it feels like being mildly drunk, or concussed. There is a sort of invisible blanket between the world and me. I find it hard to take in what anyone says. Or perhaps, hard to want to take it in. It is so uninteresting. Yet I want the others to be about me. I dread the moments when the house is empty. If only they would talk to one another and not to me."

"Love bears all things, believes all things, hopes all things, endures all things. Love never ends." -I Corinthians 13:7-8

"When the heart weeps for what it has lost, the soul laughs for what it has found." -

"We are healed of a suffering only by experiencing it to the full."

As Seen Through the Eyes of Others

Grief is a powerful force that can shake even the strongest person. The confusion, chaos, and inner turmoil that result can sweep you away from productivity and plans.

"The risk of love is loss, and the price of loss is grief--but the pain of grief is only a shadow when compared with the pain of never risking love."

"You will lose someone you can't live without, and your heart will be badly broken, and the bad news is that you never completely get over the loss of your beloved. But this is also the good news. They live forever in your broken heart that doesn't seal back up. And you come through. It's like having a broken leg that never heals perfectly--that still hurts when the weather gets cold, but you learn to dance with the limp.

"I should know enough about loss to realize that you never really stop missing someone--you just learn to live around the huge gaping hole of their absence."

"Grief I've learned is just love. It's all the love you want to give but cannot. All of that unspent love gathers up in the corners of your eyes, the lump in your throat, and in that hollow part of your chest. Grief is just love with no place to go.

"Grief is like the ocean; it comes on waves ebbing and flowing. Sometimes the water is calm, and sometimes it is overwhelming. All we can do is learn to swim

An image of a man swimming, which can symbolize grief, loss, bereavement, or grieving- sometimes we need to just keep swimming

"There is a sacredness in tears. They are not the mark of weakness, but of power. They speak more eloquently than ten thousand tongues. They are the messengers of overwhelming grief, of deep contrition, and of unspeakable

"Guilt is perhaps the most painful companion to death."

"Those who have suffered understand suffering and therefore extend their hand."

"There are no happy endings.

Endings are the saddest part,

So just give me a happy middle

And a very happy start."

A Light in the Attic

"Sometimes, only one person is missing, and the whole world seems depopulated."

"The darker the night, the brighter the stars,

The deeper the grief, the closer is God!"

"It's the kind of heartache you can feel in your bones."

"Happiness is beneficial for the body, but it is grief that develops the powers of the mind

"I think I'll miss you forever, like the stars miss the sun in the morning

Prominent as an author the tonalities, and regular people are all susceptible to personal grief. The sentiments of love lost, mortality, and brokenness are motifs that grace the pages of storybooks and religious tomes alike. It can be helpful to witness the ways that other people have framed this experience as you work through your own grief. I hope that you use these thoughts to find light in the shadows, to find joy in the sorrow, and to find peace throughout your day. Because

"Grief is the price we pay for

"While grief is fresh, every attempt to divert only irritates. You must wait till it be digested, and then amusement will dissipate the remains of

"Tears are the silent language

A mother and her adult daughter together, remembering their loved ones. Once the grief, loss, bereavement, or grieving process subsides, fond memories remain.

Uplift Your Sadness with These Grief Quotes Today

Source: pexels.com

"Believe me, every heart has its secret sorrows, which the world knows not, and oftentimes we call a man cold, when he is only sad."

Advice from Grief

Sometimes our source of light comes from unexpected places in times of loneliness and darkness. If you are in a season of grief, witnessing the experiences of other people's journeys - even in written form - can be helpful. Although you must chart your own course of recovery from grief, you can find solace in these inspiring quotes and words from great thinkers who have felt the way you feel now.

"Don't grieve. Anything you lose comes around in another form."

"Grief is the last act of love we can give to those we loved. Where there is deep grief, there was great love.

"No matter how long it's been, there are times when it suddenly becomes harder to breathe I have learned that

"When someone you love dies, and you're not expecting it, you don't lose her all at once; you lose her in pieces over a long time--the way the mail stops coming, and her scent fades from the pillows and even from the clothes in her closet and drawers. Gradually, you accumulate the parts of her that are gone. Just when the day comes--when there's a particular missing part that overwhelms you with the feeling that she's gone, forever--there comes another day, and another specifically missing part."

"To spare oneself from grief at all cost can be achieved only at the price of total detachment, which excludes the ability to experience had to endure pain and burn it as fuel for our journey

"Grief never ends… But it changes.

It's a passage, not a place to stay.

Grief is not a sign of weakness, nor a lack of faith…

"That's all it takes. The smallest reminder and in an instant, it feels like your stomach has fallen thirty stories and crashed into the steel roof of a truck. Loss is cruel like that; the days you think you're finally past it are the days it will punish you most."

"The reality is that you will grieve forever. You will not 'get over' the loss of a loved one; you will learn to live with it. You will heal, and you will rebuild yourself around the loss you have suffered. You will be whole again, but you will never be the same. Nor should you be the same, nor would you want to."

"A feeling of pleasure or solace can be so hard to find when you are in the depths of your grief. Sometimes it's the little things that help get you through the day. You may think your comforts sound ridiculous to others, but there is nothing ridiculous about finding one little thing to help you feel good in the midst of pain

As a woman lookout of her rainy window. She is lost in thought during the grief, loss, bereavement, and grieving period

"Deep grief sometimes is almost like a specific location, a coordinate on a map of time. When you are standing in that forest of sorrow, you cannot imagine that you could ever find your way to a better place. But if someone can assure you that they themselves have stood in that same place, and now have moved on, sometimes this will bring hope"

From the Bible

"Blessed are those who mourn, for they will be comforted."

Jesus in Matthew 5:4

"Suffering produces endurance, and endurance produces character, and character produces hope."

Romans 5:3-4

"What we suffer now is nothing compared to the glory He will reveal to us later."

Romans 8:18

"He will wipe away every tear from their eyes, and death shall be no more, there will no longer be any mourning, crying, or pain, for the old order of things have passed away."

Revelation 21:4

Seeking Help

Grief can undermine your ability to cope with daily activities. The nature of grief varies based on its many sources. From paralyzing flashbacks to sad memories, grief assaults your physiological and psychological wellbeing.

Grief can be very overwhelming. It haunts every waking hour.

A grief or bereavement counselor can help you process grief and loss in healthy ways.

I was a person that listens intently, focuses on issues, and then helps find successful strategies to deal with those issues. Never once did I feel that

74

she was judging me or talking down to me. She was easy for me to open up too, she was professional, and she took me seriously. Together we discussed issues of loss and grief from the passing of my father, which had become more than I could handle alone. She not only validated my feelings of loss, but she also helped me find ways to mitigate.

Learning to Go On....

"Without you in my arms, I feel an emptiness in my soul. I find myself searching the crowds for your face. I know it's an impossibility, but I cannot help myself," and "It's possible to go on, no matter how impossible it seems."

Joy and grief: the paradox and wisdom of finding joy alongside grief

I had to explore grief: how I have been able to find joy alongside deep grief, the challenges and what it has it taught me.

Joy and grief

When you see joy beside the agony, you have the keen vision of a Soul warrior.

Joy is my word of the year for 2018. I shared the beginning of my story of working with 'joy' here. when isn't what I expected. Though I knew it was never going to be an easy or straightforward journey. Reflecting on this past year, I've found the journey of exploring joy falls into themes or stages around the quarters of the year of finding joy…

This post explores finding joy alongside deep grief and how the two can co-exist. A focus of the first quarter of 2018, this theme and learning has continued through-out this year in different ways. It's been an undercurrent that I continue to work with even now

The challenge of choosing joy

But I chose the word joy because I wanted more of it in my life. It's a word often associated highlighted just how far I felt from feeling joy. Even the concept of 'enjoying' life in any way can seem challenging when you are caring for another

Joy and grief

Finding joy alongside deep grief

Balancing even the thought of joy with grief was hard in practice especially at the start of the year.

The statement I wrote down, in line with my word of the year, was: "I am unapologetically joyful." When it came to my turn to stand up, I just froze. I couldn't get the words out. The tears came and the room,

Even, through tears, I was able to say the words, "I am unapologetically joyful ". I felt immediately stronger claiming joy, if also very fragile. It demonstrated the enormous tension that lies in the juxtaposition of grief and joy. I began to have a deeper sense that day of how challenging this paradox of grief and joy might be.

It's like we are drawn into a binary view of the world, not allowing ourselves to feel joy in any way when we are in deep sadness and pain. I realized finding joy, playfulness, fun, laughter and happiness again against a backdrop of deep grief was not going to be easy. But it felt central to this year's journey.

joy and grief

The paradox of joy and grief

A big learning this year is that it's okay to feel the joy of everyday things at the same time as we feel immense pain. We tend to make it an either/or, saying to ourselves either I feel grief or I feel joy. I cannot feel both. It can feel like a terrible tension and betrayal of our pain if we feel good in any way. And feeling joy or lighter feelings can somehow feel like a betrayal of a particular person and their memory. It as if we feel we need to stay in a certain emotional space to honor that person. In this, we can deny ourselves positive feelings and experiences that can help us move through the grief and loss. Over time, this can set in and become habitual and the min

For me, joy and grief is a kind of paradox and polarity we can work with, one that does rock our beliefs but brings wisdom in its wake.

Difference between joy and happiness

Happiness thing to say about that too in her piece, The difference between joy and happiness. And why it helps to know.

Herein lies the heart of the matter. The key thing is it is not about a mutually exclusive choice between feeling grief or joy. It's not about the more fleeting feelings of happiness either. Learning to navigate the paradox of feeling joy and grief at the same time is a journey of wisdom.

Consciousness is not an either/or equation. It's about both.

The capacity to expand into both — the awareness of your joy in all circumstances — is so much of what it means to evolve…

Happiness is like rising bubbles — delightful and inevitably fleeting.

Joy is the oxygen — ever present....

Joy is the fiber of your Soul....

This means that it's possible to grieve with your whole heart, and still sense your joy. You can feel rage, and be aware of joy waiting patiently for you to return, and take deep comfort in that.

Lessons from joy and grief

So this year has been full of heart-felt lessons about joy and grief.

It's been full of learning to live in paradox and seeing joy as a kind of oxygen. This learning set the tone of the first quarter of the year as I moved through the deep grief of losing my mother. As people who have been there will know, it's a defining moment of your life. At the same time, I also experienced my job being deleted and becoming redundant So there were layers of different kinds of grief I was working through all at the same time.

I learnt it was okay to feel joy – celebrating the joy of my mother's beautiful life, the strength that lives on in me, my female ancestry and lineage, her loving kindness and knowing she was cheering me on as always as I moved into a new phase of life. All of these qualities and the simple pleasures of water, light, tea, sun, reading, it helped me much at this time.

Grief and joy can co-exist. By weaving one with the other, the passage through is deeply felt but somehow more sure-footed and grounded. Being able to smile and embrace the full gamut of emotions simultaneously is a wholehearted learning joy has taught me.

This first part of the year set the tone. It taught me that joy is often found in the smallest moments that we allow ourselves to feel even as we feel great sorrow. The light of joy can shine gently into the shadows of our sadness helping us find pockets of positive reflections to sustain us and move

Grief and pain can be our most important teachers – a wholehearted story

Never too old – finding courage and skill to empower your dreams

How I plan to manifest energy joy and intention to make the most of the coming year.

CHAPTER 3:

GETTING THE SCARS OFF

FROM NOW ON I DONT LET ANYTHING TROUBLE ME FOR I BEAR MY BODY SCARS THAT SHOWS THEY BELONG TO JESUS I JUST THANK GOD FOR MY SCARS AND WOUNDS MY SCARS ARE SIGNS OF MY SURVIVAL. THEY SHOW MY STRENGTH AND BRAVERY IN ORDER FOR ME TO CONTINUE TO REBUILED MYSELF SO I MAY BE ABLE TO BREATH AGAIN AND BE ABLE TO FACE ANOTHER DAY MY SCARS THAT I HAVE IT TELLS IS MY STORIES MY EXPERIENCE WHAT I HAVE GONE THROUGH EVERY MOMENT OF MY LIFE THAT HAS BEEN SHAPED INTO THIS WHOLE NEW CREATION IT HAS REDEMED ME AND IT HAD MADE ME WHOLE IN THE EYES OF THOSE WHO HAS SEEN MY SCARS.

AND MY STRUGGLES, MY SCARS AND WOUNDS IS ALWAYS GOING TO BE WITH ME BUT ON THING ABOUT IT IAM HAPPY TO TALK ABOUT IT AND NOT PRESSURED THIS IS A PART OF A WOUND AND SCARS THAT HAS CHANGED THE WAY THAT I SEE MYSELF. I HAD MORE EXTRA TIME, EXTRA DAYS EACH ONE WAS MY GIFT MY WOULDS SCARS, MY DOWNFALLS TRIALS PAIN SUFFERING I HAD TO INWRAP THEM, STOP AND STARE I HAD TO LAUGH AND I HAD TO LINGER LONGER I HAD TO LOVE MORE AND LOVE WELL I HAD TO ASK GOD FOR IT AND I HAD TO RECEIVE IT MY SCARES LIKE I SAID BEFORE REMINDER AND THEY ARE

UNPLEASANT THEY ARE MY SCARS.

AND THEY ARE FOR A REASON TO ME I OFTEN GO THROUGH GOD, GOD COULD HAVE MADE SCARS SO THAT IT WOULDNT SCAR WHEN YOU HEAR FOR AN EXAMPLE YOUR TONGUE HAS CERTAIN TYPES OF TISSUE THAT DOES NOT SCAR WHEN TORNED IN FACT THE TONGUE DO NOT HAVE SCAR TISSUE IT DOESENT MATTER HOW MANY TIMES YOU BIT YOUR TONGUE AND HURT YOURSELF GOD FIXES IT VIRTUALLY REPAIR IT AND IT LEAVE NO SCARE NOW EVERYONE HAVE SOME KIND OR SORT OF PHYSICAL SCAR ON OUR BODY FROM WOUNDS TO SURGICAL CUTS ACCIDENTS ITS ALL ABOUT EMOTIONAL SCARES ALL NOW ALL SCARS ARE NOT PHYSICAL ITS EASY TO SEE PHYSICAL SCARES AND WOUNDS YOU CAN SEE OLD AND NEW AND THERE ARE SOME WOUNDS. YOU JUST CANNOT SEE AND THAT IS EMOTIONAL WOUNDS THOSE ARE THE ONE YOU NEED TO HEAL THATS A HUT TO YOUR SOUL YOU SEE WHEN I HELD ON TO THE SITUATION TRAUMA THOUGHTS GRIF IT WAS TO ME A MIND SET AND IT HAD STARTED DAMANGING ME THAT WAS UNPLEASENT.

AND IT CONTINUE TO REMIND ME OF THE PAIN AND HURT MY TRIAL AND MY TRIBULATION HAVE YOU EVERY BEEN TO A BUSY SCENE AND IT WAS BUSY SCHOOL CARS THE SPEEDING OF CARS ALL THE MOVEMENT TRAFFIC ALL OF THIS IS OBVIOUS EASILY SEEN AND HEARD BUT THER IS MORE BEHAND AND BENEATH THE LOUD HUMAN ACCTIVITY ITS THE INVISBLE ACHES IN THE BIBLE JOB CALLS THEM GROANS TO ME. THIS IS A VERY GOOD WORLD. THE HEBREW IN TERM SUGGEST THAT GROAN COMES FROM WOUNDED

AND JOB IN THE BIBLE PREHAPS WOUNDED AND JOB IN THE BIBLE PREHAPS HE HAD A GOOD REASON TO ADD THIS LINE TO A POETIC FORM THE SOUL OF THE WOUNDED CRY OUT.

NOW IF YOU DONT UNDERSTAND WHAT IM SAYING ABOUT WOUNDED COME FROM A TERM CALLED PIERCED BUT IT IS NOT REFERRED TO A PHYSICAL STABBING FOR IT IS THE SOUL THAT MEAN CRYING OUT IN ISAIAH 43:1:3 DONT BE AFRAID IVE REDEEMED YOU IVE CALLED YOUR NAME. YOUR MINE WHEN YOUR OVER YOUR HEAD, ILL BE THEIR WITH YOU, WHEN You're in ROUGH WATER, YOU WILL NOT GO DOWN WHEN YOUR BETWEEN A ROCK AND A HARD PLACE, IT WONT BE A DEAD END.

BECAUSE IAM GOD YOUR PERSONAL GOD. BLOODY AND PAINFUL THAN BODY STABBING NOW IF YOU AS I CONTINUE TO SPEAK OF THOSE HEARTS HAVE BEEN BROKEN OR THOSE WHO SUFFER FROM THEBLOWS OF THE SOUL STABBING NOW IF YOU LOOK AT THIS THE CITY IS FULL OF SUCH SOUNDS OF WOUNDS OF THE WOUNDED BRUSING AND BROKEN CRYING OUT OF GROANS FROM THE HEART THIS IS ME I AM DESCRIBING LIVING WITH MEMORIES THING THAT HAD HAPPEN TO MY DAUGHTER WHICH CAN THESE WOUNDS STAYED.

IN RED AND TENCER MY WOUNDS IS DEEP BECAUSE IT PIERCED ME SO DEEPLY THE BLOW CAME FROM ME THAT I TRUSTED AND RESPECTED AND THAT MY HURT WAS BROUGHT BY THE TONGUE SO EVERTHING THAT I WHEN THROUGHT WITH LAFRESHIA HYDROCEPHLUS I HAD TO STAY AND LET IT BLEED FROM THE INSIDE AND LET IT PASS IF YOU GO BACK TO YOUR BIBLE AND I WILL TAKE YOU.

THERE IF YOU WOULD TURN TO THE OLD TESTAMENT TO THE BOOK OF ZECHARIAH. THE 13 CHAPTER AND IN THIS CHAPTER IM GOING TO GO THEIR WITH YOU THE MOST INTERESTING VERSE 1 IN CHAPTER 13 AND 6 VERSE OF ZECHARIAN AND HE SHALL ANSWER THOSE WHICH SAY UNTO HIM, WHAT ARE THE WOUNDS IN THY HANDS AND HE SHALL ANSWER THOSE WHICH I WAS WOUNDED?

IN THE HOUSE, CHAPTER 13 OF ZECHARIAH IS A PROPHECY OF THE SECOND OF JESUS CHRIST AND THE BIBLE THAT TEACHES WHEN JESUS CHRIST COME AGAIN WHO`RE GOING TO SAY WITH HIM, WITH AMAZEMENT THEY ARE GOING TO BE ASTOUNDED THEY`RE GOING TO ASK THE RISEN RETURNING SAVIOR WHAT ARE THE WOUNDS IN YOUR HAND/ THE NAIL PRINTS WILL STILL BE THERE AFTER TWOTHOUSAND YEARS THE NAIL PRINTS ARE STILL AND HE WILL ANSWER THAT WHERE I WAS WOUNDED IN THE HOUSE OF MY FRIENDS DID YOU KNOW THIS IN THAT RESSECTED GLORIFIED BODY THE LORD JESUS CHRIST SCARS OF HIS CRUCIFIXION STILL REMAINS NOW IM GOING TO TAKE YOU BACK TO JOHN THE 20 CHAPTER AFTER JESUS CHRIST HAD TO COME OUT THE GRAVE AND DOUBTING THOMAS SAID I DONT BELIVE HE HAS BEEN RAISED FROM THE DEAD JEASUS APPEARED AND JEASUS SAID TO THOMAS, TAKE YOUR FINGER AND PUT IN THE NAIL PRINT, PUT YOUR HAND IN THE WOUND IN MY SIDE AND DONT BE FAITHLESS, BUT BE BELIEVING AND THOMAS SAW THE SCARS IN THE GLORIFIEDBODY OF JESUS HE FELL TO HIS KNEES AND SAID, MY LORD, MY GOD, THOSE SCARES OF JESUS ARE IN THE GLORIFIED BODY IN HEAVEN AND WHEN HE COMES AGAIN HE WILL BRING THOSE SCARS WITH HIM THE ONLY MAN MADE THINGS IN HEAVEN ARE

THE SCARS OF JESUS AND THEY ARE ALL THERE FOR ALL ENTERITY.

Sign of healing

When my daughter died my world was different and uncrowned to think of grief as an adjustment to life loss while feeling certain feeling I knew it was expected this is my journey the emotion that I had experience was normal even if they weren't expected I had to allow myself to feel each as it arise and I had to understand that it will take some time to adjust to my new circumstances in revelation 21:4. He will wipe away every tear from their eyes and death shall be no more neither shall there be mourning nor crying nor pain anymore for former things has passed I found alone was a process to navigate alone this is my journey in psalm 147 :3 he heals the brokenhearted and binds up there wounds I've learned to remember that whatever emotion you are feeling was a part of my process to me there was no right way or wrong way to feel roman 8:18 for I consider that the suffering of this present time are not worth comparing with the glory that is to be revealed to us.

Acceptant was not necessarily a permanent state nor did it mart a return for me to return to happiness or the pre loss state of my mind the death of my daughter had changed the circumstances of the world for me I have to accept the mark of my understanding as well of my willingness to move forward in life the pain will ease over time for me but the loss will always be with me. One's attitude towards death is central to any healing process although it is frequently ignored it is always in the background no one actually wants to face the possibility of death or even the idea of death the real healing has come out of some kind of openness when I realize what was happening I picked up the spirit buoyancy I thought of sanity develops to present the possible of facing my loss my healing was my magical sense as so Jesus my healer had to put his hands on me for me to miraculously to heal me the important thing to me it was real the healing without taking medicine and talking to some kind of therapy god came in and healed me. You see a scar is a wonderful sign of healing my scar reveal the mystery of life that God is greater than death and destruction and the wounds you experience my open wounds it begins to heal that which it has formed out of my fibroblast cells which are devoid of fat as fibroblasts send out filaments connection is made which causes the open wound to shrink and then to close as the tissue forms closing the wound, it open leaves scars tissue. If you google scares you can find ways to minimize or make them less noticeable over the time mad fade and be less prominent logically scars are proof the body to healed this is a wonderful thing I don't want to go through life with an open infection wound but I know that god had to let me remember the scars is a sign of his power though I can never go back and undo the past I have to keep moving forward by embracing the truth he has chosen for me all of my scars are a mystery of my life that god is greater and the wounds that I have experience was for me to focus when I gave thanks and thoughts swirl that's in my head the emotional scar all it was the privilege to praise the lord.

The testament of grace has become my testimony to the lord s grace and his deepest compassionate love for me the lord has healed my wounds but he left the scars and it was a reminder of how merciful I was I was broken and I was torn apart but the lord took my heart and he healed the wound and left the scar I know god is with me in my pain and in my fear in my lioness. I know he said he will never leave me or forsake me god is my healer of my broken heart in Isiah 53:5 but he was wounded for our transgressions he was abused for our inequalities the chastisement of us peace was upon him and with his stripes we are healed, I have experience death with my eldest child this that is complicates different situation the death of my child often comes as a mother this loss is an experience it affected me it made me feel the lack of control of myself was a complicate of loss though she was my child. This is just like in Luke 8:40:42 in Luke 40 now when Jesus returned a crowd welcome him for they were all expecting him 41 then a man named jabirus a ruler of the synagogue came and fell at Jesus feet pleading with him to come to the house42 because his daughter a girl of about twelve was dying as Jesus was on his way the crowds almost crushed him…. 49 while Jesus was speaking someone came from the house of juries the synagogues ruler your daughter is dead he said don't bother the teacher anymore now the exposition is when tragedy sticks with no warning crashing down upon us it happens. At heart all the capacity.

GOD I THANK YOU FOR MY WOUNDS AND SCARS

I know that my wounds are my story that will use I am so thankful the pain I have gone through it was like waking up to a new sunrise and having to look back on the other side it's like dark water that was in my deepest pain it just causes brokenness but I'm so grateful for my scars because without the scars I wouldn't ever know my hearty did not know god plan.

My scars reminded me of something it reminded me of the unpleasant my scars are there because of the death and for each for each one of my scars it has indicated that something bad has happened most of my scars has indicated or received from something bad when I received a scar on my body it is there for a reason I often though god could have made flesh so it would not scar. I know that scars will not always appear at the very moment of the event that causes the scar it takes a while for the scar to appear scars physical scars on the outside are the one thing but the scars both emotional and spiritual on the inside are something else in fact the inward scars are much more serious the inward scars usually do not come until much later in life the inward scars affect me but it can it gave me more reason to continue to walk with god there was I would love to forget but the scars will be there forever it is a constant reminder as painful as they may these inwardly do serve a very important purpose my scares reminded me to learn that is life my life is my scars.

I have learned that my skin was torn it never healed automatically now there is a different in infected wound and a wound of a broken heart. Now any medical doctor will tell you that the infected wound is serious and the skin can break into the skin and lets in dangerous bacteria and infectious organism set in but god give us a physical healing process that we can even see for yourself and he give us a physical healing process that we can even see yourself god has given us an emotional and spiritual healing process to asset us with the scar of life I know that scars of life is difficult to deal with though we try to move through it intense. The scars that I had help me now if you look at it Paul her in the text viewed it we come to a conclusion that God will not look at your resume god will not ask you what kind of experience you have he will not look at the degree's diploma but he will look at your scars.

This is how I believed Paul viewed his scars he knew that Christ suffered for him Paul is willing to suffer foe Christ and suffer he did he bore as much as any man or woman had to bear for Christ 2 Corinthian 11:24;25 of the Jews five times received I forty stripes save on 25 thrice was I beaten with rods once stoned thrice I suffered shipwreck a night and a day. I have been in the deep. However, despite the physical appearance these scars served a purpose his scared a power sermon his scares told a true story that no one can deny Jesus scars reprinted the facts that all things work for the good isn't that amazing there was a trial in my life and at that time, I didn't understand why the fire and the flames do you remember job he didn't understand either and he lost more than man or woman will ever loose but his endurance despite the wrong counsel of sisters and despite the ill advice passed out by his so called friends despite Satan releasing his hounds to buffet and batter job at every turn job endured the scars on Paul's body were the marks of Christ just like the cattle but since god has never given up on me I will surely not give up on him this symbolic who bear the scar of Jesus Christ.

Now I have to look at the line and the marks of me journey the common wisdom call the light of Gods purpose they are my beautiful trophies. God has a purpose and a plan for my scares and me that means the bible says that god knits us together in us mother's womb that mean that god made my daughter with holes in it also means that god chose for my daughter to be born in a time when medical technology has developed and a place where it was available to fix my heart he decided that my daughter I would bear and he knew that I would not abandon her no matter what condition she was in you see I have scars to remind me every day of just how much god loves me Jesus had scars when he rose from the grave Thomas needed proof he needed to see the scars in Jesus hand and side these scars part of evidence to prove that the resurrection was not a figment of his imagination brought about grief denial.

You can take any number of actions to find meaning in your life. Many people begin new hobbies or return to old ones. Others take on opportunities to be of service. Some become better at their vocation, confirming their delight in doing something they love to do. In this way a person participates in redefining life. Thankfully, the Lord has provided that your loss does not diminish who you are: your personality and your place in His kingdom. However, YOUR world HAS changed! Your place in it has changed. Like an intricate mobile that has lost one of its weights, you experience a jangling, jarring tossing until the new balance is found, and slowly the bouncing settles down. There is balance, but it is a new configuration.

The Lord designed your spirit to seek and eventually achieve this balance. His loving care is always lifting you, countering the depressing effects of your loss. The warmth of His love continually radiates in your spirit. The process of grief is designed to bring your consciousness out of the cold and dark of loss into His presence again. You again take on the responsibility to live your life to its fullest potential.

My stages of grief are predictable but not uniform. They vary among circumstances and people. You have at hand a number you understand what is going on and explain why you feel the anger, despair, sadness, emptiness and pain. The Lord, especially through His Word, allows you to experience the feelings even as He alleviates them. The angels in your life, the loved ones who walk with you, hold you up when your knees buckle. There are many books and pieces of music that salve our wounds. Use them all, and your particular and unique grief process will proceed to a conclusion the Lord has designed just for you in the time He has provided.

Comfort from words of scripture

"What words from scripture have brought you comfort in a difficult time

"Nothing is permitted unless some good may come of it

"The Lord is in control of everything. If I give over control to Him and allow myself to be carried along in the stream of Providence, I will see how the Lord is providing for me and my happiness

"Trust in the Lord, and do good; dwell in the land, and feed on His faithfulness." (Psalm 37: 3)

"This verse has helped me see a way forward when it has been hard to move on from grief and loss. The first part is to trust that the Lord will be with you through your loss. The practical advice to "do good" is especially healing—when I engage in an activity which helps others it helps me realize that I still have a use to perform, and it definitely feeds my soul."

"The Lord is always with me, in dark times and in happy ones."

"Peace I leave with you; my peace I give you. I do not give to you as the world gives. Do not let your hearts be troubled and do not be afraid." (John 14:27)

"How close the Lord is to us, really powerful in times of self-doubt and inner turmoil."

".... Even though I walk through the valley of the shadow of death, I will fear no evil, for you are with me, your rod and staff, they comfort me." (The 23rd Psalm)

"Some of the most comforting words of peace and promise at the time of separation from a loved one."

"Then the Lord answered Job out of the storm. He said: Who is this that darkens my counsel with words without knowledge?... Where were you when I laid the earth's foundation?... Can you bring forth the constellations in their seasons or lead out the bear with its cubs...." (Job 38)

"The whole book of Job is worth reading but I especially like chapter 38 when God Answers Job. It gave me a way to accept and cope with my sorrow. It made me realize that I must trust the Lord's providence and not expect to understand or have an overview of everything that happens. I am not God; I must accept that He takes care of things.

There's a kind of grief which you can never really get over completely, but you can learn to live with positively on a daily basis. It's the grief of having a disabled child. When our baby was just a few days old, we discovered that she had a medical problem – severe epilepsy – that was likely to lead to lifelong physical and mental disability.

an uplifting image for the grief of having a disabled child

Grief for a Disability includes Shock and Guilt

The initial feelings were of shock and disbelief – this was the sort of thing that happened to other people, wasn't it? At first, I found it very difficult to grieve – I was too tied up in the hospital procedures and diagnostic tests, trying to understand what was happening.

Then the fear set in – the fear that I wouldn't be able to cope physically and, more worryingly, emotionally with caring for a profoundly disabled child. After that, the guilt – for resenting that my life would never again be my own, that freshia almost certainly never live independently

Grief for My Intellectually Disabled Daughter

We will always grieve for the child that might have been. We will never know what it is to have a simple conversation with her – she is non-verbal

Finding the Positive in Grief

I think that most people who find themselves in a situation like this will astonish themselves at how much positivity they can find. We were told freshia never walk – we researched physical therapy methods, invested a lot of time and effort, and we now have a young lady who can walk and even run, although her balance is not the best.

We never gave up hope of finding a specific diagnosis, even though the odds were stacked against us. It took ten years, and numerous blood tests, but we learned that freshia had genetic disorder affecting the transmission of messages between brain cells.

The First Difficult Years of Grieving for a Disabled Child

The first two to three years were by far the hardest to deal with emotionally. I think it takes time to accept the version of "normality" which you come to recognize as your own. I held back my tears when I went to the postnatal classes and saw how all the other babies could raise their heads, but freesia's. I smiled at the platitudes: "they all develop in their own time".

The grief must have been present under the surface most of the time, but what I remember now, looking back after almost thirteen years, are specific incidents, such as:

The realization that, because of the localization of the seizures within her brain, freshia never learn to speak, understand language, or read. As a child I loved reading, I still do, and the thought that freshia never be able to take herself to a fantasy world simply by looking at the words on a page left me utterly distraught. But, undeterred, I have always read to her, and she loves books. I don't know whether she understands every word, but she loves the pictures, the rhythm of my voice, the made up monster sounds, and she laughs along with me.

Be Proud of Every Step of Hard Won Progress

It would be easy to become lost in a lifetime of grief, but what you learn to do is to see the positive in every little step of progress. Everything has been much harder won for her than for an "ordinary" child, and I am immensely proud of her tenancy

An answer to a prayer

When we lose a loved one to the lord, you have indeed lost at least for no. but that child has gained and so has almighty. Philippians 1:20:23 we may shed enough tears to fill the buckets but those streams enough tears running down our cheeks will listen with joy- when we realize that our loved one's death is nothing less than to an answer to the almighty prayer. The death of my daughter, my loved on, in the lord may present on of the greatest of faith. I can trust my loved that my loved one is better now off with the beloved. Will we have believed that the almighty is reaping the fruit of his work for sinners? If we do, then our grief, and almighty will turn our sorrow into great joy, john 16:20 "Precious in the sight of the lord in the death of his saints" psalm 116:15 and it can be for us too. We cling to the hope that death will never win 1 Corinthian 15:54:55. The almighty grieved himself so we will never have to endure hopeless grief in the face of death. Afreshia I will hold you again, 2 Samuel 12:15:23 of all of the death that of a child is the most unnatural and hardest to bear we expect the old to die while that kind of separation is always difficult it comes as no surprise but the death of a child young or old or even a youth is a different matter.

Life is beauty wonder and potential lies ahead of them death is accrued thief when it strikes down in a way that is different from that child bones of that parent and the flesh of their flesh when that child dies part of that parent is also buried as of me I had to burial 2 children's when I lost my children the affect was widespread it touched name as a mother as caregiver in a unique way in the scripture there is a story that offered me some insight and comfort as I share in my grief. David and Bathsheba little boy lived for seven days. the reminder is that we can be recalled life when it is brief is a reminder that all of us can be recalled at any time life is transitory. each man`s life is a breath" psalms 39:9 since we have no guarantee of how long god chooses to grant life we must maximize the opportunities god gives us count every day a blessing blesses every day by counting. now responding to the grief until I found the relief the illness and death of David child teaches us how to respond in grief until we find relief there must be the expression of grief it must do its work he did not try to bury his feeling grief is a felt response it must not be smoothened David made a mistake in his grief he tried to grieve along a grief shared it is a burden divided rejoiced with them that do rejoice and weep with them that weep. Romans 12:15 time brought me healing but it did not heal all of my wounds. time did not heal for me it was what did with the time that healed me...... along life or a short life are the equal importance to God. If we bury our grief it would be like toxic water and it will surface again and the contamination will make more trouble. time alone doesn't overcome sorrow, because to me sorrow is a neutral it's like a vacuum therefore, we have to turn to the only one who can enable us to deal with our grief god. the lord is close to the brokenhearted and save those who are crushed in spirit psalm 34:18 faiths in Jesus Christ who is the resurrection and the life gives us unexpected strength we grieve but not as those who have no hope. Now David felt assured of his child`s presence in heaven and also that he would be there as well David had sinned he was accountable. why did he have hope? psalm 51 is the

94

eloquent expression of David expression sin and guilt. he sought God's forgiveness, and he received it. the scripture is so clear" whosoever shall call upon the name of the lord shall be saved" roman 10:13 this child is in the lord presence by his grace and through Jesus Christ we will get there too. as I recognize the sovereignty of god the death of my child was recognize the sovereignty of god that growing awareness bring the rest to spirit god loves children's scripture clearly illustrates his. hoping that Jesus might touch them people has brought babies to him when the disciples saw this they tried to send them away. but Jesus said to the disciples "let these children alone don't get between them and me these children are kingdom's pride and joy mark this unless you accept god's kingdom in simplicity of a child, you'll never get in" Luke 18:16:17.

When my child died I struggled with the purpose and will of god and I know that I had purpose in the divine design in writing about that brief life and grief god created Lafreshia to live 30 years since he came and brought her back home with her she is now living eternal where I may be surprised to find me true calling which always seemed just out the reach here on earth. God released Lafreshia until we are rejoined finally, we ask god to give us peace as we seek to release this child until we are rejoined David said "I bring him back again I will go to him but he will not have returned to me " 2 Samuel 12:23 David's response and insight carries penetration truth for us the scripture tells us that he went to the house of the lord and worshiped comforted his wife and returned to the business of life. 2 Samuel 12:20:29.

This child has brought joy and taught us so much about the precious gift of a child though grief hammered at our hearts and the memories will always be cherished we realize because Jesus Christ and his victory over death that there will be a reunion it has been a year that my daughter Lafreshia has been gone and she left a sunshine but I turned on the headlights and I am still going on.... and Lafreshia I shall keep on doing my best until that glorious day when I can see you again it is signed and signed with love no name just a simple testimony to go to the faith that enable person to go on in the face of sorrow and death.

Lafreshia until that day come to that day when all mysteries, purpose, and plans of god are sorted for me in the day when we can see gods face let us be so thankful that life has enriched and made me better because of it. Lafreshia was my beautiful child who spend thirty years with me and overcoming all of obstacles when she went to be with the lord I was truly blessed by her amazing life and I just want to say these words to my beloved Lafreshia as I have looked back on all the years you brought me so much joy freshia I wouldn't change a thing you have taught me how to appreciate life you have taught me to be the caring mother that I am now Lafreshia now you can dance with David and fish with peter I just cannot imagine a life so pleasant and neater when I look back and draw a conclusion the conclusion that I have drowned it was me my child I got the longest straw. now my child belongs to god. today I have released her hand as god has grasped them over there and she will never have to suffer again god will never let her go the key to my child casket is in the hands of the son of god and he will come some morning and use it.

God is the alpha and the omega says the lord god who is and who was and who is to come the almighty revelation 1:8 freshia my elderly daughter has passed way and I wrote this for her in her memory it is called Lafreshia his hand print it is interesting and it was a life experience and a stage of grief to reflect of how I felt when my daughter passed away Lafreshia was my elder daughter she was born with complication you were lying in my arms and I tried to say goodbye it might have been the best they said but I know it was a lie as I gazed at your hand print that was given to me each and every day I know to this day that you will never have to fill no more pain Lafreshia all I wanted to say you fought for every breath you took trying not to let go my love Lafreshia until that day that one day that god made you his leaving me below Lafreshia although you couldn't walk nor talk nor could you count to ten your life was so precious god had a meaning for your life, your life had more impact than a hundred million men's. from your mother you had a time in this world you always kept a smile on your face you never showed no pain no suffering it was always joy not to only me but to everyone especially Claudia you will always be remembered by all Lafreshia. I gave you that name for a reason and that reason was that one day I knew you would be free that day came Lafreshia and god said I'm going to give you your wing baby girl you can now fly with my angels and you are free I love you Lafreshia.

I want to pray not only for me for all those that are still grieving and that are still grieving over someone and still to this day that have not gotten over a loved of a child father god in heaven my grief for all those that are still grieving and still grieving over their loved ones I pray that you would comfort them with the comfort them with the comfort that you give father god I pray that you would send supportive people into not just my life send people into other lives father you have the last word in everything and we trust you in any kind of word I know lord that you will not put no more on us that we cannot bear father god I ask to take all of this pain and grieving away not for me for all of those that are still grieving so they will know that they don't have to carry this load of a burden on them and that they will not have to go through this alone mostly lord I pray for a sense of your presence lord help me and those to meditate in what is true lord help them to know that you are the father that cares for his children deeply I know lord that every time we shed a tear you are saving each tear that everyone has shredded I pray lord in your name to touch us in order for us to continue to move on in your name, Amen.

JOHN 16:33 I HAVE TOLD YOU THESE THINGS, SO THAT IN ME YOU MAY HAVE PEACE. IN THIS WORLD

YOU WILL HAVE TROUBLE. BUT TAKE HEART! I HAVE OVERCOME THE WORLD.

I want to pray not for only me for all those that are grieving and still grieving over someone and still to this day have not gotten over a loved one or a child Father God in heaven I pray for not for my grief but for all the grieving ones I pray that you would comfort them with the comfort that you give father god I pray that you would send supportive people into not just my life send people in others life so they know that they don't have to carry this burden alone but mostly I pray for the sense your presence helps them to meditate on what is true lord help them to know that you are the god and you care deeply for them so much you are saving each tear that everyone had or done shredded I pray this lord in you name.

In conclusion of writing this story many don't understand or even realize that hydrocephalus is the most common reason for brain surgery in babies and children's and yet there is still less funding for this research or a care for the chronic condition even after treatment many faced repeat of surgeries in resulting. demised qualities of life in my case my daughter these facts are sad and has been ignored and still to exposers. This book cries only a mother hears is one of my powerful books this book I've written have saved me and my heart mind and my soul this is a true gift from my heart it has set me free to know that my daughter is set free to be with our father up above all the sobbed tears of a feuded mother. My book solved my soul it helped me by writing, it helped me to breath and it also helped me to also change the way I have grievances to the stream pain terrible loss was indiscernible the emotions lost is like no other one often misunderstood by many I had to remember the good days are harder than I could image compassion and love not advice that inside a look why there was so much loss of grief the lifetime is needed I had to go to the inside and I had to take a very good look at a child I felt was lost only those who have walked the path of a child loss understand the depth and breadth have learned that my fears and tears was a trekking though the unimaginable I learned that love never dies there will be a day hour minute and a second I will stop thinking about my child all the circumstances of who I am and how different some are there is no greater bond than connections between daughter and a mother that understand the agony of enduring the death of a child it's the pain that I have suffered through my life time unfortunately was a life time thing nothing will ever be the same again.

I have to keep moving on there is no bow no fix no solution there I am no glue for my broken heart no exile for my pain no going back in time for as long as I breath I will be in pain and grief and I will have those aches and pains for my daughter simply because I gave birth. With all of my soul it will never be time where I won't think about this is an irrevocably altered forever everyday as a mother moving the mountain in the honor of my daughter that has left too soon its starts movements the most powerful force on this earth and the love between my child is the lifetime to behold this grief was reckoned it was to me like an empty chair room space that I thought would become less space that would become less empty this empty space like a family picture the empty is vacant forever gone for this life time empty space that should be full everywhere I go there will and will always be a missing place in my heart that missing space is my life it will always be there forever a hold in my heart time do not take place in a space that is less empty neither do platitudes clinches I had to stop dwelling on well intentional nothing does no matter how you look how I looked at it empty is still empty missing is still missing gone is still gone the problem is nothing can fill it minutes after minutes' hour after hour day by day hour by hour second by second day after day year after year heart breaking years the empty space remains that empty space.

Still I'm missing my child that's a lifetime quite as contrary in fact through it took a while for me to get here I live from a much deeper place I love deeper still because I grieve I also know a joy like no other the joy I experience now is far deeper and now more intense than the joy I have experience before my life it is such an alchemy of grief because I've clawed my way from the depth of unimaginable pain suffering and all the sorrow over and over again when I know joy comes however and whenever it does it will be the joy that reverberates through my pores of my skin and every bone in my body I feel it all over deeply but the love that is my pain it really my joy that I can embrace on and I thank every morsel of it my life is now more rice and vibrant and full not deceit my loss but because of it in my grief it is my gift sometime many of my gift don't in a way make sense and in another way it makes it worth it.

I am grateful beyond words for each and every day every gift that comes to me and comes my way I have to bow my head to each day to my lord up above and say thank you lord because there is nothing and I mean nothing absolutely nothing I take for granted living life in this way gives me greater joy than I have ever known possible and I have my daughter to thank the best gift forever been given to me and to say this even death can't take that away Matthew 5;4 says blessed those who mourn, for they will be comforted when I lost my child I was in a turmoil me life was turned upside down it was stricken from me I really didn't know if I would every see the light again the multifaceted response to the loss particularly to the loss of someone that you were bonded to the suffering of my child left me all alone it destroyed me the bible explained to me the importance of God's word even though I walk through the valley of the shallow of death.

I will fear no evil, for you are with me; your rod and your staff, they comfort me. The happiness's that I have now is from the lord who want above all else to follow his footsteps when I walk through the valley of weeping it will become a place of springs where pools of blessing and refreshment collect after rains they will grow constantly in strength and each of them is invited to meet the lord god is my comfort blanket his love is still sufficient now that I have gotten to a place where I am grateful for two deposit in haven I have been through dark times and I have survived what I didn't know it was total blackness and it was ahead. Making my decision and the extra thoughts that I took was making my decision to have my child and deciding forever to have my heart go walking around outside my body the tolerate that I had was my trivia my laugh was my lunacy and my care was my cry and all of that together was my talc my tender loving care.

SPIRITUALITY

On the days when I missed my son the most, I was desperate to find something to comfort me. I spent hours searching for things to make me feel better – TV shows, music, food, shopping, reading, anything. When I searched for scriptures, I rarely found bible verses that I as grieving parents.

After a lot of reading and studying the word, I finally wrote down and stuck in a mason jar. Whenever I need a message to uplift me, I pull one out and reflect on God's word and his promises to his people. The bible verses below have comforted me in my darkest hours

I love the Lord, for he heard my voice; He heard my cry for mercy. Because he turned his ear to me, I will call on him as long as I live. The cords of death entangled me, the anguish of the grave came over me; I was overcome by distress and sorrow. Then I called on the name of the Lord: "Lord, save me!"

The Lord is gracious and righteous; our God is full of compassion. The Lord protects the unwary; when I was brought low, he saved me. Return to your rest, my soul, for the Lord has been good to you. For you, Lord, have delivered me from death, my eyes from tears, my feet from stumbling, that I may walk before the Lord in the land of the living.

Psalm 116:1-9

The Lord is the everlasting God, the Creator of the ends of the earth. He will not grow tired or weary, and his understanding no one can fathom. He gives strength to the weary and increases the power of the weak. Even youths grow tired and weary, and young men stumble and fall; but those who hope in the Lord will renew their strength.

They will soar on wings like eagles; they will run and not grow weary, they will walk and not be faint.

Isaiah 40:28-31

I will lift my eyes up to the mountains – where does my help come from? My help comes from the Lord, the Makes of heaven and earth. He will not let your foot slip – he who watches over you will not slumber.

The Lord watches over you – the Lord is your shade at your right hand; the sun will not harm you by day, nor the moon by night. The Lord will keep you from all harm – he will watch over your life; the Lord will watch over your coming and going both now and forevermore.

Psalm 121: 1-3, 5-8

Rejoice always, pray continually, give thanks in all circumstances; for this is God's will for you in Christ Jesus.

1 Thessalonians 5:16-18

Truly my soul finds rest in God; my salvation comes from him. Truly he is my rock and my salvation; he is my fortress, I will never be shaken.

Psalm 62:1-2

For no one is cast off by the Lord forever. Though he brings grief, he will show compassion, so great is his unfailing love. For he does not willingly bring affliction or grief to anyone.

Lamentations 3:31-32

So do not fear, for I am with you; do not be dismayed, for I am your

God. I will strengthen you and help you; I will uphold you with my righteous right hand. For I am the Lord your God who takes hold of your right hand and says to you, do not fear; I will help you.

Isaiah: 41:10, 13

Humble yourselves, therefore, under God's mighty hand, that he may lift you up in due time. Cast all your anxiety on him because he cares for you. And the God of all grace, who called you to his eternal glory in Christ, after you have suffered a little while, will himself restore you and make you strong, firm and steadfast. To him be the power for ever and ever. Amen.

1 Peter 5:6-7, 10-11

Trust in the Lord with all your heart and lean not on your own understanding; in all your ways submit to him, and he will make your paths straight.

Proverbs 3:5-6

For I know the plans I have for you," declares the Lord, "plans to prosper you and not to harm you, plans to give you hope and a future. Then you will call on me and come and pray to me, and I will listen to you. You will seek me and find me when you seek me with all your heart.

Jeremiah 29:11-13

And as a bonus, this is my personal favorite:

Have I not commanded you? Be strong and courageous. Do not be afraid; do not be discouraged, for the Lord your God will be with you wherever you go.

Joshua 1:9

favorite bible erases that provide you comfort as a grieving parent

Asking for Strength

SPIRITUALITY

We have heard the popular phrases, "Lord, help me," or "Jesus take the wheel," indicating that we need some form of strength to get us through something. But when we really talk to God and ask for strength, how do we know that we have it?

The last time I asked God for strength, I wanted Him to let me know when I got it, like a confirmation email or something. Kind of like how I track a package with UPS and make sure I leave a signature once it's delivered.

What I didn't realize is that with

Strength is discovered when you go through something. That's how you know that you got the [strength] juice.

When you ask God for strength, you have to be prepared for the storm that shows you how strong you really are. Without the test, how do you determine how strong you are? There's no measuring cup or Fitbit strength tracker for that, boo.

How many times have you been caught in a really bad situation and asked, "why me?" Remember the strength you prayed for and then ask yourself, "why not me?" Strength is a gift, and its God's way of saying, "I got you."

There is a reason for every trial and tribulation, and I encourage you to appreciate the hardships just as much as you enjoy the triumphs, for they show you how strong you really are.

How to Choose Faith Over Fear?

Fear is one byproduct of modern life that we just can't avoid. Our jobs are often in jeopardy, are under stress, and struggle with social pressures we could not even have imagined at their age. Let's face it, the world is a dangerous place. These stressors, have produced an age of unprecedented anxiety. products, to cope with the fear. But for people of faith, the Bible remains a source of comfort in those troubled times when we are overwhelmed by fear and feel as if the walls are closing in on us.

The people of the Bible had to face their fears, too. The Israelites wandered 40 years in the blistering wilderness, facing hostile enemies on all sides and often having to survive with very little food. The disciples of Jesus faced the fear of persecution, during and after his lifetime. Sometimes they succumbed to it, but often their faith saw them through and enabled them to deal with the sometimes violent opposition to their new faith.

Psalm 34:4–5

"I sought the Lord, and he answered me and delivered me from all my fears. Those who look to him are radiant, and their faces shall never be ashamed."

Take your fears to the Lord and He will transform your life

Truly it all seemed impossible.

I told the Lord I would do anything He told me to, but when He actually gave the instructions, I was terrified. I began to talk myself out of what God was saying. I told myself maybe I was just making it up in my mind, or perhaps this was something I should pray about and wait a while longer so I could get more information, more details, and have more time to grow, prepare, and learn.

If God would reveal His plan then I could move forward in faith, but I allow fear to hinder my actions. I hold onto what I know and see, and I miss what God is orchestrating.

When God told Jonah to go to Nineveh, God gave Him specific instructions. "Get up, go to Nineveh, and cry out." (Jonah 1:2) God provided a clear three-step process. He clearly told Jonah what to do, where to go, and how to speak. You would think if the details were spelled out so clearly, Jonah would have no problem following the instructions.

But instead of getting up and going to Nineveh, Jonah exerted his energy by fighting against the very purpose God designed.

It's easy to look at Jonah and shake our heads. If he only knew about the storm that would rise up causing him to compromise his life as a direct result of his disobedience.

The instructions God gave him seemed clear to me, but we know Jonah had other things in mind. Perhaps questions, fear, and doubt consumed him so much that he was willing to give up his life to pursue his own direction.

When it comes to us and our instructions, it begins to get complicated because we, just like Jonah, exhaust ourselves questioning God, doubting our skills, and forgetting everything we heard from God in the first place. As we run from God's designed plan, we struggle and we fight. The question is how long will we run?

God has instructions for you and for me. I believe He spells them out clearly, yet we miss it by over-analyzing the details. We begin to feel like we could never succeed at the very thing God has called us to.

We begin to believe we must have misinterpreted what we heard in the first place. We obsess over the possibility of failure and we fight the very purpose God designed for us by trying to do everything in our own power. When we don't succeed, we become frustrated, feeling like we are spinning our wheels and not fulfilling our true purpose in life

God has a call for each one of His children. No one is excused or excluded from the instructions God freely offers. God could have easily chosen someone else as soon as Jonah ran the wrong way, but He pursued Jonah for the specific purpose of Nineveh even after Jonah jumped ship. How beautiful the mercy of our mighty Savior!

If you know God called you to do something for His kingdom and somewhere along the way frustration, and confusion has set in, it's time to return to the instructions you once heard. Just like Jonah was given a second chance to go to Nineveh, many times God gives us a second chance too.

If God is calling you:

1. Don't run the wrong way. Run to God.

Draw near to God, and he will draw near to you. Cleanse your hands, you sinners, and purify your hearts, you double-minded. James 4:8(ESV)

2. It's not time to have fear. It's time to have faith.

When I am afraid, I put my trust in you. Psalm 56:3

But without faith it is impossible to please him: for he that cometh to God must believe that he is, and that he is a rewarder of them that diligently seek him. Hebrews 11:6(KJV)

3. You can't do it alone. You need God's presence.

The LORD your God is in your midst, a mighty one who will save; he will rejoice over you with gladness; he will quiet you by his love; he will exult over you with loud singing. Zephaniah 3:17

4. It's not impossible. All things are possible with God.

Jesus looked at them and said, "With man it is impossible, but not with God. For all things are possible with God." Mark 10:27

Having faith in God's call does not mean you completely erase every fear from your heart and mind. It means you take the first step no matter if your knees are knocking, your heart is palpitating, and your hands are shaking like a leaf. So go ahead. It's time to take the step that God has instructed you to take. It's time to do what you know God is telling you. Take the leap. Jump into the deep end and don't look back.

When we finally choose obedience, we will see God's hand at work. It might be the most difficult thing we have experienced. It might be a lot of hard work, and it might be that we see God in way we have never seen Him before. God's power is available to each of us and His instructions are clear.

1. Get up.

2. Go.

3. Tell others.

Whatever it is that God is calling you to do, He will give you what you need to succeed.

Being confident of this very thing, that he which hath begun a good work in you will perform it until the day of Jesus Christ. Philippians 1:6(KJV)

What are you waiting for? Choose faith over fear.

When a child has special-needs that require constant caretaking, the supportive family finds itself defined by the unconditional love it gives and receives. When the child dies, the family suffers not only the loss of the child, but the loss of an intense and focused way of life.

Suffering from this compounded grief, parents need support to find ways to redirect the constant love, energy, and attention given their child for what may have been a short time or many years.

By necessity, the families of special-needs children lead lives that are-to a greater or lesser degree-different from those of society's mainstream. Since the relationship with the child is unique, it follows that the grief process will also be unique.

Parents often feel grief when they first learn their child is disabled-feelings born in the ashes of hopes and dreams of what will never be. Depending on the depth of a parent's expectations, this grief can be devastating.

Parents often feel resentment and anger during the child's life. Being stripped of dreams for the child's future may lead to feelings of resentment. Anger can result from the constant caretaking and worry that go hand in hand with having a special-needs child. The daily struggle to make a child's life as fulfilling as possible often takes its toll.

The onslaught of guilt is normal. During the lifetime of a special-needs child, it is common for parents to feel guilt over not having enough time to develop a satisfying and deep relationship with the child's siblings or time to spend nurturing the spousal relationship. By necessity, a disabled or special needs child's needs take precedence over just about any other aspect of family life. Other forms of guilt may arise when questioning the source of the condition that disabled the child. Many parents worry that they are somehow responsible or were the source themselves. It is important to remember that guilt is an emotion-it doesn't have to make sense or be logical.

After a child dies, parents may agonize over the fact they didn't see the death coming-or that they did anticipate the death but didn't do enough to save the child. Most parents of a special-needs child are aware that the child may suffer an early death and do all they can to prevent or delay it. But when death does occur, parents often second-guess themselves with questions like "Why didn't I sense that my child's death was so near? If I had, maybe I could have done something more!"

When the child dies, parents sometimes feel a sense of release and even relief. This, too, can bring feelings of tremendous guilt. I loved my child they may think. How can I feel relief that he or she is dead? Stepping back and looking closely at these feelings, parents may realize that psychologically it is normal to feel a sense of relief that the child is no longer in pain, and that the huge responsibility to protect the child from harm has ended. Guilt can sometimes be lessened by remembering how much of the parents' lives were devoted to assuring that the child experienced the best life possible.

During their child's lifetime, parents often feel isolated. Most parents of special-needs children find the average parent cannot understand the depths of despair, joy, love, and sadness that are an integral part of living with a disabled or special needs child. These feelings of isolation, of not being understood, often continue after the child's death. Though the parents' sorrow may be overwhelming, friends, acquaintances, and even some family members might express thoughts such as, "I know you must feel happy your child is in a 'better place' and isn't in pain any longer," or "I know how much you loved him, but your life was never your own. Now you can go out at night or even take a vacation without feeling guilty." Although certainly well-meaning, remarks such as these which because pain come from an ignorance of the family's special love for this child.

Grief and pain may not be validated by those who cannot understand that sharing life with a special-needs child has huge rewards that accompany the work and worry. Discussing the rewards experienced as a result of sharing life with a disabled child may be met with blank, uncomprehending stares. Only others who have experienced a similar lifestyle may be able to understand.

Parents of special-needs children tend to develop a strong sense of protectiveness and responsibility, and in return receive unconditional love. It is normal for all parents to assume the difficult and sometimes overwhelming responsibility of protecting and watching over the safety of their children. For a non-special-needs child, this responsibility is most concentrated in the child's younger years. The intense desire felt by parents to keep their special-needs child safe, however, does not diminish as the child ages. It goes on and on. It is, in part, this endless need to nurture that forges the tensile bonds of love and caring, creating a family with a central focus that is, by necessity, the special-needs child. It is the death of the child and the abrupt loss of this focus that compound the grieving process.

Addressing Support Needs for Families

The pain of a family grieving the loss of a special-needs child may be best shared with and validated by someone who understands the unique lifestyle the family has led, someone who can connect with a statement such as, "I feel pain every time I look at the empty place where we always stored his wheelchair." The Compassionate Friends welcomes as members any family experiencing the death of a child, and those suffering the loss of a special-needs child

Where Do Special-Needs Families Go from Here?

Families that have experienced years of intense personal and loving one-on-one support for a special-needs child suddenly find themselves with an emptiness in their hearts. Yet the need to give unconditional love continues. Where do they go to put these nurturing skills to work? What do they do now?

Unfortunately, there are many special-needs children who do not have families. Great courage is required to consider giving a home to another special-needs child after suffering the death of one so beloved, but this is an option that can be carefully weighed, knowing that the giving of unconditional love allows the return of unconditional love. When someone we love dies...we are changed. When that someone is our child...we are changed forever, deeply, no matter how old they were. Letting go is not a possibility. Everything in my being was geared to hold on, to protect and to be aware of his life. It didn't matter that he was an adult, twice the size of me. Past, present and future collapsed into a series of knows. This event shook me to my core

IN CONCLUSION

IN CONCLUSION OF WRITING THIS STORY MANY DONT UNDERSTAND OR EVEN REALIZE THAT HYDROCEPHALUS IS THE MOST COMON REASON FOR THE BRAIN SURGERY IN BABIES AND CHILDREN.

AND YET THEIR IS STILL VERY LITTLE FUNDING FOR THIS REASEARCH OR A CURE FOR THIS CHRONIC CONDITION EVEN AFTER TREATMENT MANY FACED REPEAT OF SRUGERIES IN RESULTING DIMINISHED QUALITY OF LIFE IN THIS CASE OF MY DAUGHTER THESE FACTS ARE SAD AND IGNORED AND STILL TO THIS DAY ITS IS STILL BEING IGNORED AND IT WILL REMAIN SO WITHOUT GREATER EXPOSERS. THIS BOOK THAT I HAVE WRITTEN ON MY DAUGHTER BEHALF IS AND STILL A BIG ISSUE IT IS VERY CHALLENGING AND DIFFICULT ITS A LOT OF PAIN AND SUFFERING THAT MY DAUGHTER HAD.

HYDROCEPHLUS IS A DEFECT AND IT IS AN ON GOING PROCESS IT IS ALSO A DAY TODAY PROBLEM AND THIS PROBLEM LEADS UP TO HYDROCEPHALUS IT IS NOT A DISEASE AND THERE IS NO CURE SO ALL TO SAY THIS IS WRITING THIS STORY WAS THE HARDEST THING FOR ME AND IT WAS THE HARDEST THING I HAD TO DO IN ORDER FOR ME TO LET ALL THIS STUFF GO I HAD TO ABUNDANT LIFE AND JESUS TEACHES US AND PROMISED US.

IN JOHN 10:10 JESUS SAID, THE THEIF DOES NOT COME EXCEPT TO STEAL, AND TO KILL AND DESTROY.

I HAVE COME THAT THEY MAY HAVE A LIFE OF ABUNDLY". UNLIKE A THEIF, THE LORD JESUS DOES NOT COME FOR

SELFISH REASON. HE COMES TO GIVE, NOT TO GET IN HE COMES THAT PEOPLE MAY HAVE LIFE IN HIM

THAT IS MEANINGFUL, PURPOSE, JOYFUL, AND ETERNAL. WE RECEIVE THIS ABUNDANT LIFE THE MOMENT WE ACCEPT HIM AS OUR SAVIOR.ONE THING THAT OCCURED TO ME IN MY MIDST OF MY HARD TIME MY IDEA FOR

LOOKING TO GOD STRENGTH IN THE MIDST OF HARD TIMES THESE ENCOUAGE CHALLENGES THAT I FOUND AND NEEDED FOR MY STRENGTH IN THE MIDST OF MY TURBULENT TIMES AS I FOUND MY STRENGTH IN GOD.

SOMETIME GETTING UP IN THE MORNING CAN BE THE HARDEST THING YOULL DO ALL DAY WHEN LIFE WORRIES PRESS YOU DOWN ON YOU AND TAKE YOUR SOUL HOSTAGE, THE MOST IMPORTANT THING YOU CAN. DO FOR YOURSELF IS TURN TO GOD. HE WILL ALWAYS BE THERE FOR YOU THROUGH THE GOOD TIMES AND THE BAD TIMES AND THIS WAS THE TIME I NEEDED TO SHARE THIS STORY CRIES ONLY A MOTHER HEARS.

AND IM GOING TO LEAVE THIS VERSE WITH YOU, JOHN 16:33 I HAVE TOLD YOU THESE THINGS, SO THAT IN ME YOU MAY HAVE PEACE. IN THIS WORLD YOU WILL HAVE TROUBLE. BUT TAKE HEART! I HAVE OVERCOME THE World `

I WANT TO THANK ALL THAT HAVE BEEN BY MY DAUGHTER LAFRESHIA SIDE THROUGH ALL OF HER TRIALS & TRIBULATIONS.

CLAUDIA KINADE THANKS FOR ALL THE SUPPORT abundant life for being there

MRS KAREN BISHOP AND LATE DAVID BISHOP FOR ALL YOUR SUPPORT AND ALSO STANDING BY US.

MR.REX NICHOLSON THANKS FOR YOUR TIME AND YOUR SUPPORT.

THANKS FOR ALL OF YOU.

AND LAST MY MOTHER EARNESTINE GREEN MY MOM PASSED AWAY JULY 4 2017 RIGHT AFTER I FINISHED LAFRESHIA STORY. MY MOM WAS THE GREATEST PERSON IN OUR LIFE LAFRESHIA

GRANDMOTHER WAS THE GREATEST MOTHER AND GRANDMOTHER YOU COULD POSSIBLE HAVE SHE WAS THEIR FROM THE TIME LAFRESHIA WAS BORN UNTILL LAFRESHIA TURNED THIRTY YEARS OLD AND I WILL AND LAFRESHIA FOR SURE WILL MISS HER AND LAFRESHIA WILL LOVE AND ALWAYS BE GRATEFUL.

FOR MY MOM AND THE GRANDMOTHER, SHE WAS FOR JUST STEPPING UPI THE WAS SHE DID TO HELP.

AND THE OF ALL THE SUPPORT SHE HAVE GIVE US MAY GOD BE WITH HER I THANK YOU MOTHER RIP.

1949 TO 2017 YOU WILL ALWAYS BE LOVED AND IN OUR HEARTS. WE LOVE YOU MOTHER.

www.ingramcontent.com/pod-product-compliance
Lightning Source LLC
Chambersburg PA
CBHW071013120626
46546CB00003B/1063

* 9 7 8 1 9 5 7 6 1 8 5 0 0 *